# BABY DOLL

# Baby Doll

THE SCRIPT FOR THE FILM BY

# TENNESSEE WILLIAMS

INCORPORATING THE TWO ONE-ACT PLAYS

WHICH SUGGESTED IT

27 Wagons Full of Cotton

The Long Stay Cut Short/or/The Unsatisfactory Supper

A NEW DIRECTIONS BOOK

Book design by Stefan Salter. Manufactured in the United States of America by American Book–Stratford Press, New York. New Directions Books are published by James Laughlin. New York Office—333 Sixth Avenue.

PUBLISHER'S NOTE:

For a number of years Elia Kazan, the director of several of Tennessee Williams' plays on Broadway as well as films, had been urging Mr. Williams to weld into an original film story two of his early one-act plays which were, roughly, concerned with the same characters and situation. And in the summer of 1955, while he was traveling in Europe, Mr. Williams wrote and dispatched to Mr. Kazan a proposed script, quite different from the two short plays. With some changes this was filmed the following winter mainly in the Mississippi rural area which had been the original setting of the two short plays.

Although he had himself adapted several of his Broadway successes for films, this was Mr. Williams' first original screen play. Many who came to read it, including his publishers, felt that although few "shooting" scripts have ever been published, this one was publishable as it stood. To add further interest to the volume, it was decided to include the two one-act plays from which BABY DOLL sprang, *27 Wagons Full of Cotton,* previously published by New Directions in a volume of short plays under this general title, and *The Long Stay Cut Short/or/The Unsatisfactory Supper,* published by The Dramatists' Play Service, to whom New Directions is grateful for permission to republish it here.

The film, *Baby Doll,* which was previously announced as *The Whip Hand* and *Mississippi Woman,* was produced and directed in the winter of 1955–1956 by Elia Kazan for Newtown Productions, Inc., and is released by Warner Brothers. The principal roles are filled by Carroll Baker, Eli Wallach, Karl Malden and Mildred Dunnock.

1]

INTERIOR. DAY.

*A voluptuous girl, under twenty, is asleep on a bed, with the covers thrown off. This is* BABY DOLL MEIGHAN, ARCHIE LEE's *virgin wife. A sound is disturbing her sleep, a steady sound, furtive as a mouse scratching, she stirs, it stops, she settles again, it starts again. Then she wakes, without moving, her back to that part of the wall from which the sound comes.*

2]

INTERIOR. DAY. CLOSE SHOT. BABY DOLL.

*She is a little frightened of what sounds like a mouse in the woodwork and still doesn't sound like a mouse in the woodwork. Then a crafty look.*

3]

INTERIOR. DAY. FULL SHOT.

*She gets up, as the sound is continuing, and moves stealthily out of her room.*

**4]**

HALL. DAY. FULL SHOT.
*She comes out of her room and just as stealthily opens
the door to an adjoining room and peeks in.*

**5]**

CLOSE SHOT. BABY DOLL.
*Astonished and angry at what she sees.*

**6]**

WHAT SHE SEES. ARCHIE LEE MEIGHAN.
*He is crouched over a section of broken plaster in the
wall, enlarging a space between exposed boards with
a penknife. Unshaven, black jowled, in sweaty pajamas.
On the bed table behind him is a half-empty bottle of
liquor, an old alarm clock, ticking away, a magazine
called* Spicy Fiction *and a tube of ointment. After a
moment he removes the knife and bends to peer through
the enlarged crack.*

**7]**

CLOSE SHOT. BABY DOLL.
BABY DOLL:
Archie Lee. You're a mess.

**8]**

ARCHIE LEE.
*He recovers.*

*Page 8*

BABY DOLL.

BABY DOLL:

Y'know what they call such people? Peepin' Toms!

FULL SHOT. ARCHIE LEE'S BEDROOM.

ARCHIE LEE:

Come in here, I want to talk to you.

BABY DOLL:

I know what you're going to say, but you can save your breath.

ARCHIE LEE:

(*Interrupting*)

We made an agreement . . .

BABY DOLL:

You promised my daddy that you would leave me alone till I was ready for marriage. . . .

ARCHIE:

Well?

BABY DOLL:

Well, I'm not ready for it yet. . . .

ARCHIE:

And I'm going crazy. . . .

BABY DOLL:

Well, you can just wait. . . .

ARCHIE:

We made an agreement that when you was twenty years old we could be man and wife in more than just in name only.

BABY DOLL:

Well, I won't be twenty till November the seventh. . . .

ARCHIE:

Which is the day after tomorrow!

BABY DOLL:

How about your side of that agreement—that you'd take good care of me? GOOD CARE OF ME! Do you remember that?! Now the Ideal Pay As You Go Plan Furniture Company is threatening to remove the furniture from this house. And every time I bring that up you walk away. . . .

ARCHIE:

Just going to the window to get a breath of air. . . .

BABY DOLL:

Now I'm telling you that if the Ideal Pay As You Go Plan Furniture Company takes those five complete sets of furniture out of this house then the understanding between us will be canceled. Completely!


## 11]

ARCHIE LEE.  AT WINDOW.

*He is listening. We hear the distant sound of the Syndicate Cotton Gin. Like a gigantic distant throbbing heartbeat.* ARCHIE LEE *puts the window down. He crosses to the mirror, dolefully considers his appearance.*

BABY DOLL:

Yeah, just look at yourself! You're not exactly a young girl's dream come true, Archie Lee Meighan.
*The phone rings downstairs. This sound is instantly followed by an outcry even higher and shriller.*

BABY DOLL:

Aunt Rose Comfort screams ev'ry time the phone rings.

ARCHIE:

What does she do a damn fool thing like that for?

*The phone rings again.* AUNT ROSE COMFORT *screams downstairs. The scream is followed by high breathless laughter. These sounds are downstairs. Archie Lee exits.*

BABY DOLL:

She says a phone ringing scares her.


12]

HALL.

ARCHIE *lumbers over to a staircase, much too grand for the present style of the house, and shouts down to the old woman below.*

ARCHIE:

Aunt Rose Comfort, why don't you answer that phone?


13]

DOWNSTAIRS HALL.

AUNT ROSE *comes out of the kitchen and walks towards the hall telephone, withered hand to her breast.*

AUNT ROSE:

I cain't catch m'breath, Archie Lee. Phone give me such a fright.

ARCHIE:

(*From above*)

Answer it.

*She has recovered some now and gingerly lifts the receiver.*

AUNT ROSE:

Hello? This is Miss Rose Comfort McCorkle speaking. No, the lady of the house is Mrs. Archie Lee Meighan, who is the daughter of my brother that passed away . . .

ARCHIE LEE *is hurrying down the stairs.*

ARCHIE:

They don't wanta know that! Who in hell is it talking and what do they want?

AUNT ROSE:

I'm hard of hearing. Could you speak louder, please? The what? The Ideal Pay As——

*With amazing, if elephantine, speed,* ARCHIE *snatches the phone from the old woman.*

ARCHIE:

Gi'me that damn phone. An' close the door.

*The old woman utters her breathless cackle and backs against the door.* ARCHIE *speaks in a hoarse whisper.*

ARCHIE:

Now what is this? Aw. Uh-huh. Today!? Aw. You gotta g'me more time. Yeah, well you see I had a terrible setback in business lately. The Syndicate Plantation built their own cotton gin and're ginnin' out their own cotton, now, so I lost their trade and it's gonna take me a while to recover from that. . . .

*(Suddenly)*

Then TAKE IT OUT! TAKE IT OUT! Come and get th' damn stuff. And you'll never get my business again! Never!

*They have hung up on him. He stands there—a man in tough trouble. Then abruptly starts massaging his exhausted head of hair.*

AUNT ROSE:

(*Timidly*)

Archie Lee, honey, you all aren't going to lose your furniture, are you?

ARCHIE:

(*Hoarse whisper*)

Will you shut up and git on back in the kitchen and don't speak a word that you heard on the phone, if you heard a word, to my wife! And don't holler no more in this house, and don't cackle no more in it either, or by God I'll pack you up and haul you off to th' county home at Sunset.

AUNT ROSE:

What did you say, Archie Lee, did you say something to me?

ARCHIE:

Yeah, I said shoot.

*He starts upstairs.*

AUNT ROSE *cackles uneasily and enters the kitchen. Suddenly, we hear another scream from her. We pan with her, and reveal* OLD FUSSY, *the hen, on top of the kitchen table pecking the corn bread.*

14]

UPSTAIRS HALL.

ARCHIE *is heading back to his bedroom.* BABY DOLL *appears in a flimsy wrapper at the turn of the stairs crossing to the bathroom.*

BABY DOLL:

What made her holler this time?

ARCHIE:

How in hell would I know what made that ole woman holler this time or last time or the next time she hollers.

BABY DOLL:

Last time she hollered it was because you throwed something at her.

*She enters bathroom.* ARCHIE LEE *stands in doorway.*

ARCHIE:

What did I ever throw at Aunt Rose Comfort?

BABY DOLL:

*(From inside bathroom)*

Glass a water. Fo' singin' church hymns in the kitchen. . . .

*We hear the shower go on.*

ARCHIE:

This much water! Barely sprinkled her with it! To catch her attention. She don't hear nothing, you gotta do somethin' to git the ole woman's attention.

*On an abrupt impulse he suddenly enters the bathroom. Sounds of a struggle. The shower.*

BABY DOLL:

Keep y'r hands off me! Will yuh? Keep your hands off . . . Off.

ARCHIE LEE *comes out of the bathroom good and wet. The shower is turned off.* BABY DOLL'*s head comes out past the door.*

BABY DOLL:

I'm going to move to the Kotton King Hotel, the very next time you try to break the agreement! The very next time!

*She disappears. . . .*

15]

CLOSE SHOT.   ARCHIE LEE WET.

DISSOLVE.

16]

ARCHIE LEE.

*He is seated in his 1937 Chevy Sedan. The car is caked with pale brown mud and much dented. Pasted on the windshield is a photo of* BABY DOLL *smiling with bewilderment at the birdie-in-the-camera.*

ARCHIE LEE *is honking his horn with unconcealed and unmodified impatience.*

ARCHIE:

*(Shouting)*

Baby Doll! Come on down here, if you're going into town with me. I got to be at the doctor's in ten minutes.

*(No answer)*

Baby Doll!!!

*From inside the house.* BABY DOLL'*s voice.*

BABY DOLL:

If you are so impatient, just go ahead without me. Just go ahead. I know plenty of ways of getting downtown without you.

ARCHIE:

You come on.

*Silence. The sound of the Syndicate Gin.* ARCHIE *does a sort of imitation. His face is violent.*

ARCHIE:

Baby Doll!!!

BABY DOLL *comes out on the sagging porch of the*

*mansion. She walks across the loose boards of the porch through stripes of alternate light and shadow from the big porch pillars. She is humming a little cakewalk tune, and she moves in sympathy to it. She has on a skirt and blouse, white, and skintight, and pearl chokers the size of gold balls seen from a medium distance. She draws up beside the car and goes no farther.*

ARCHIE:

You going in town like that?

BABY DOLL:

Like what?

ARCHIE:

In that there outfit. For a woman of your modest nature that squawks like a hen if her *husband* dast to put his hand on her, you sure do seem to be advertising your——

BABY DOLL:

*(Drowning him out)*

My figure has filt out a little since I bought my trousseau AND paid for it with m'daddy's insurance money. I got two choices, wear clo'se skintight or go naked, now which do you want me t'——

ARCHIE:

*Aw, now, hell! Will you git into th' car?*

*Their loud angry voices are echoed by the wandering poultry.*

BABY DOLL:

I will git into the rear seat of that skatterbolt when you git out of the front seat and walk around here to open the door for me like a gentleman.

ARCHIE:

Well, you gonna wait a long time if that's what you're waiting for!

BABY DOLL:

I vow my father would turn over in his grave. . . .

ARCHIE:

I never once did see your father get out and open a car door for your mother or any other woman. . . . Now get on in. . . .

*She wheels about and her wedgies clack-clack down the drive. At foot of drive she assumes a hitchhiker's stance. A hot-rod skids to a sudden and noisy stop.* ARCHIE LEE *bounds from his car like a jack rabbit, snatching a fistful of gravel as he plummets down drive. Hurls gravel at grinning teen-age kids in hot-rod, shouting incoherently as they shoot off, plunging* BABY DOLL *and her protector in a dust-cloud. Through the dust . . .*

ARCHIE LEE:

Got your license number you pack a——

DISSOLVE.

16A]

THE CAR INTERIOR.

*They are jolting down the road.*

ARCHIE:

Baby Doll, y'know they's no torture on earth to equal the torture which a cold woman inflicts on a man that she won't let touch her??!! No torture to compare with it! What I've done is!! Staked out a lot in hell, a lot with a rotten house on it and five complete sets of furniture not paid for. . . .

BABY DOLL:

What you done is bit off more'n you can chew.

ARCHIE:

People know the situation between us. Yestiddy on Front Street a man yelled to me, "Hey Archie Lee, has y'wife outgrowed the crib yet??" And three or four others haw-hawed! Public! Humiliation!

BABY DOLL *in back seat, her beads and earrings ajingle like a circus pony's harness.*

BABY DOLL:

Private humiliation is just as painful.

ARCHIE:

Well! —There's an agreement between us! You ain't gonna sleep in no crib tomorrow night, Baby, when we celebrate your birthday.

BABY DOLL:

If they remove those five complete sets of furniture from the house, I sure will sleep in the crib because the crib's paid for—I'll sleep in the crib or on the top of Aunt Rose Comfort's pianner. . . .

ARCHIE:

And I want to talk to you about Aunt Rose Comfort. . . . I'm not in a position to feed and keep her any——

BABY DOLL:

Look here, Big Shot, the day Aunt Rose Comfort is unwelcome under your roof . . .

ARCHIE:

Baby Doll, honey, we just got to unload ourselves of all unnecessary burdens. . . . Now she can't cook and she——

*Page 18*

BABY DOLL:

If you don't like Aunt Rose Comfort's cookin, then get me a regular servant. I'm certainly not going to cook for a fat ole thing like you, money wouldn't pay me—— Owwwwww!

ARCHIE *has backhanded her. And prepares to do so again.*

BABY DOLL:

Cut that out. . . .

ARCHIE:

You better quit saying 'fat ole thing' about me!!

BABY DOLL:

Well, you get young and thin and I'll quit calling you a fat old thing. —What's the matter now?

ARCHIE LEE *points to off right with a heavily tragic gesture.*

17]

TRAVELING SHOT. SYNDICATE GIN. THEIR VIEWPOINT.

*It is new, handsome, busy, ˥learly prospering. A sign (large) reads: SYNDICATE COTTON GIN.*

18]

TWO SHOT. ARCHIE AND BABY DOLL.

ARCHIE:

There it is! There it is!

BABY DOLL:

Looks like they gonna have a celebration!

ARCHIE:

Why shouldn't they!!?? They now got every last bit

of business in the county, including every last bit of
what I used to get.

BABY DOLL:

Well, no wonder, they got an up-to-date plant—not like
that big pile of junk you got!!

ARCHIE *glares at her.*

QUICK DISSOLVE.


19]

WAITING ROOM. DOCTOR'S OFFICE.

ARCHIE *and* BABY DOLL *enter, and he is still hotly pur-
suing the same topic of discussion.*

ARCHIE:

Now I'm just as fond of Aunt Rose Comfort——

BABY DOLL:

You ain't just as fond of Aunt——

ARCHIE:

Suppose she breaks down on us?? Suppose she gets a
disease that lingers——

BABY DOLL *snorts.*

ARCHIE:

All right, but I'm serving you notice. If that ole woman
breaks down and dies on my place, I'm not going to be
stuck with her funeral expenses. I'll have her burned
up, yep, cremated, cremated, is what they call it. And
pack her ashes in an ole Coca-Cola bottle and pitch the
bottle into TIGER TAIL BAYOU!!!

BABY DOLL:

*(Crossing to inner door)*
Doctor John? Come out here and take a look at my

husband. I think a mad dawg's bit him. He's gone ravin' crazy!!

RECEPTIONIST

*(Appearing)*

Mr. Meighan's a little bit late for his appointment, but the doctor will see him.

BABY DOLL:

Good! I'm going down to the——

ARCHIE:

Oh, no, you're gonna sit here and wait till I come out. . . .

BABY DOLL:

Well, maybe. . . .

ARCHIE *observes that she is exchanging a long, hard stare with a young man slouched in a chair.*

ARCHIE:

And look at this! Or somethin'.

*He thrusts a copy of* Screen Secrets *into her hands and shoves her into a chair. Then glares at the young man, who raises his copy of* Confidential.

DISSOLVE.

20]

INNER OFFICE.

ARCHIE LEE *has been stripped down to the waist. The doctor has just finished examining him. From the ante-room, laughter, low. Which seems to make* ARCHIE LEE *nervous.*

DOCTOR:

You're not an old man, Archie Lee, but you're not a young man, either.

ARCHIE:

That's the truth.

DOCTOR:

How long you been married?

ARCHIE:

Just about a year now.

DOCTOR:

Have you been under a strain? You seem terrible nervous?

ARCHIE:

No strain at all! None at all. . . .

*Sound of low laughter from the waiting room. Suddenly,* ARCHIE LEE *rushes over and opens the door.* BABY DOLL *and the* YOUNG MAN *are talking. He quickly raises his magazine. . . . Archie closes the door, finishes dressing. . . .*

DOCTOR:

What I think you need is a harmless sort of sedative. . . .

ARCHIE:

Sedative! Sedative! What do I want with a sedative? ? ?

*He bolts out of the office. . . .*

DISSOLVE.

21]

MEDIUM LONG SHOT. ARCHIE LEE'S CAR
GOING DOWN FRONT STREET.

BABY DOLL *sits on her side aloof. Suddenly a moving van passes the other way. On its side is marked the legend: IDEAL PAY AS YOU GO PLAN FURNI-*

*Page 22*

*TURE COMPANY. Suddenly,* Baby Doll *jumps up and starts waving her hand, flagging the van down, then when this fails, flagging* Archie Lee *down.*

22]

## CLOSER SHOT. ARCHIE'S CAR.

BABY DOLL:

That was all our stuff!

ARCHIE:

No it wasn't. . . .

BABY DOLL:

That was our stuff. Turn around, go after them.

ARCHIE:

Baby Doll, I've got to wait down here for my per-scription. . . .

*At this moment another IDEAL PAY AS YOU GO PLAN FURNITURE COMPANY goes by, in the OTHER direction.*

BABY DOLL:

There goes another one, towards our house.

ARCHIE:

Baby, let's go catch the show at the Delta Brilliant.

BABY DOLL:

*(Starts beating him)*

ARCHIE:

Or let's drive over to the Flaming Pig and have some barbecue ribs and a little cold beer.

BABY DOLL:

That's our stuff. . . !

Archie Lee *looks the other way.*

I said that's our stuff . . . !! I wanta go home. HOME.
NOW. If you don't drive me home now, I'll, I'll,
I'll—— Mr. Hanna. Mr. Gus Hanna. You live on Tiger
Tail Road . . .

ARCHIE:

I'll drive you home.

*He spins the car around and they start home.*

23]

EXTERIOR MEIGHAN HOUSE. DAY.

MEIGHAN'*s car turns in the drive. The van we saw is
backed up to the house, and furniture is being removed
from the house.* BABY DOLL *runs among them and starts
to beat the movers. They go right on with their work,
paying no attention. After a time* AUNT ROSE *puts her
arms around* BABY DOLL *and leads her into the house.*

24]

CLOSE SHOT. ARCHIE LEE.

*He really is on a spot. Again he hears the sound of the
Syndicate Cotton Gin. He makes the same sound,
imitating it, he made earlier. He looks in its direction
and spits. Then he gets out of the car and walks towards his empty home.*

25]

INTERIOR. ARCHIE LEE'S HOUSE. THE
PARLOR.

BABY DOLL *is sobbing by the window. The screen door
creaks to admit the hulking figure of* ARCHIE LEE.

ARCHIE:

(*Approaching*)

Baby Doll . . .

BABY DOLL:

Leave me alone in here. I don't want to sit in the same room with a man that would make me live in a house with no furniture.

ARCHIE:

Honey, the old furniture we got left just needs to be spread out a little. . . .

BABY DOLL:

My daddy would turn in his grave if he knew, he'd turn in his grave.

ARCHIE:

Baby Doll, if your daddy turned in his grave as often as you say he'd turn in his grave, that old man would plow up the graveyard.

*Somewhere outside* AUNT ROSE *is heard singing: "Rock of Ages."*

ARCHIE:

She's out there pickin' roses in the yard just as if nothing at all had happened here. . . .

BABY DOLL:

I'm going to move to the Kotton King Hotel. I'm going to move to the Kotton King Hotel. . . .

ARCHIE:

No, you ain't, Baby Doll.

BABY DOLL:

And I'm going to get me a job. The manager of the Kotton King Hotel carried my daddy's coffin, he'll give me work.

ARCHIE:

What sort of work do you think you could do, Baby Doll?

BABY DOLL:

I could curl hair in a beauty parlor or polish nails in a barbershop, I reckon, or I could be a hostess and smile at customers coming into a place.

ARCHIE:

What place?

BABY DOLL:

Any place! I could be a cashier.

ARCHIE:

You can't count change.

BABY DOLL:

I could pass out menus or programs or something and say hello to people coming in!

*(Rises)*

I'll phone now.

*(She exits)*

26]

HALL.

BABY DOLL *crosses to the telephone. She is making herself attractive as if preparing for an interview.*

BABY DOLL:

Kotton King? This is Mrs. Meighan, I want to reserve a room for tomorrow mornin' and I want to register under my maiden name, which is Baby Doll Carson. My daddy was T. C. Carson who died last summer when I got married and he is a very close personal friend of the manager of the Kotton King Hotel—you know—what's his name. . . .

27]

EXTERIOR OF HOUSE.

ARCHIE *comes out door and wanders into the yard, passing* AUNT ROSE, *who holds a bunch of roses.*

AUNT ROSE

Archie Lee, look at these roses! Aren't they poems of nature?

ARCHIE:

Uh-huh, poems of nature.

*He goes past her, through the front gate and over to his Chevy.*

*The front seat on the driver's side has been removed and a broken-down commodious armchair put in its place.*

*Sound of the Syndicate Gin, throbbing.* ARCHIE LEE *reaches under the chair and fishes out a pint bottle. He takes a slug, listens to the Syndicate, takes another. Then he throws the bottle out of the car, turns the ignition key of the car and . . .*

28]

THE CHEVY ROCKS OUT OF THE YARD.
                                    DISSOLVE.

29]

THE INTERIOR.  BRITE SPOT CAFE.

*A habitually crowded place. Tonight it is empty. In the*

*corner a customer or two. Behind the bar, the man in the white apron with nothing to do is sharpening a frog gig on a stone. Enter* ARCHIE, *goes over to the bar.*

ARCHIE:

Didn't get to the bank today, Billy, so I'm a little short of change. . . .

*The* BARTENDER *has heard this before. He reaches to a low shelf and takes out an unlabeled bottle and pours* ARCHIE *a jolt.*

ARCHIE:

Thanks. Where's everybody?

BARTENDER:

Over to the Syndicate Gin. Free liquor over there tonight. Why don't you go over?

*(Then he laughs sardonically)*

ARCHIE:

What's the occasion?

BARTENDER:

First anniversary. Why don't you go over and help them celebrate.

ARCHIE:

I'm not going to my own funeral either.

BARTENDER:

I might as well lock up and go home. All that's coming in here is such as you.

ARCHIE:

What you got there?

*The* BARTENDER *holds up a frog gig. The ends, where just sharpened, glisten.*

ARCHIE:

Been getting any frogs lately?

BARTENDER:

Every time I go out. Going tomorrow night and get me a mess. You wanna come? There's a gang going. You look like you could use some fresh meat.

*Another rather despondent-looking character comes in.*

ARCHIE:

Hey, Mac, how you doing?

MAC:

Draggin', man.

BARTENDER:

Why ain't you over to the Syndicate like everybody else?

MAC:

What the hell would I do over that place. . . . That place ruined me . . . ruined me. . . .

BARTENDER:

The liquor's running free over there tonight. And they got fireworks and everything. . . .

MAC:

Fireworks! I'd like to see the whole place up in smoke. *(Confidentially)*

Say, I'm good for a couple, ain't I?

*As the* BARTENDER *reaches for the same bottle-without-a-label, we*

DISSOLVE TO

30]

EXTERIOR. SYNDICATE GIN.

*A big platform has been built for the celebration and decked out with flags, including the Stars and Bars of Dixie and the Mississippi State Banner.*

*A band is playing "Mississippi Millions Love You," the
state song, which is being sung by an emotional spin-
ster. Several public officials are present, not all of them
happy to be there as the county has a strongly divided
attitude towards the Syndicate-owned plantation. Some
old local ward heeler is reeling onto the speaker's platform and a signal is given to stop the band music.* THE
OLD BOY *lifts a tin cup, takes a long swallow and re-
marks.*

THE OLD BOY:

Strongest branch water that ever wet my whistle. Must
of come out of Tiger Tail Bayou.

*There is a great haw-haw.*

THE OLD BOY:

*(Continues)*

Young man? Mr. Vacarro. This is a mighty fine party
you're throwing tonight to celebrate your first anniversary as superintendent of the Syndicate Plantation and
Gin. And I want you to know that all of us good
neighbors are proud of your achievement, bringin' in
the biggest cotton crop ever picked off the blessed soil
of Two River County.

*The camera has picked up a handsome, cocky young
Italian,* SILVA VACARRO. *His affability is not put on, but
he has a way of darting glances right and left as he
chuckles and drinks beer which indicates a certain
watchfulness, a certain reserve.*

*The camera has also picked up, among the other lis-
teners, some uninvited guests . . . including* ARCHIE
LEE *and his friend from the Brite Spot.* ARCHIE LEE *is*

*well on the way and, of course, his resentment and
bitterness are much more obvious.*

THE OLD BOY:

Now when you first come here, well, we didn't know
you yet and some of us old-timers were a little stand-
offish, at first.

VACARRO's *face has suddenly gone dark and sober. In
his watchfulness he has noticed the hostile guests. With
a sharp gesture of his head, he summons a man who
works for him—*ROCK—*who comes up and kneels
alongside. The following colloquy takes place right
through* THE OLD BOY's *lines.*

SILVA:

There's a handful of guys over there that don't look
too happy to me. . . .

ROCK:

They got no reason to be. You put 'em out of business
when you built your own gin, and started to gin your
own cotton.

SILVA:

Watch 'em, keep an eye on 'em, specially if they start
to wander around. . . .

THE OLD BOY:

*(Who has continued)*

Natchully, a thing that is profitable to some is un-
profitable to others. We all know that some people in
this county have suffered some financial losses due in
some measure to the success of the Syndicate Plantation.

VACARRO *is looking around again. Rather defiantly, but
at no one in particular. Between the knees of his cor-*

*duroy riding breeches is a whip that he carries habitu-*
*ally, a braided leather riding crop.*

THE OLD BOY:

But as a whole, the community has reaped a very rich
profit.

*He has said this rather defiantly as if he knew he was*
*bucking a certain tide. . . . A voice from the crowd.*

VOICE:

Next time you run for office you better run on the Re-
publican ticket. Git the nigger vote, Fatso!

THE OLD BOY:

*(Answering)*

Just look at the new construction been going on! Con-
tractors, carpenters, lumbermen, not to mention the
owner and proprietor of the Brite Spot down the road
there! And not to mention——

*Suddenly somebody throws something at the speaker,*
*something liquid and sticky. Instantly,* ROCK *and* VA-
CARRO *spring up. . . .*

ROCK:

Who done that? ! ? !

SILVA:

*(Crossing to front of platform)*

If anybody's got anything more to throw, well, here's
your target, here's your standing target! The wop! The
foreign wop!!

*Big rhubarb.* THE OLD BOY *is wiping his face with a*
*wad of paper napkins.*

*Suddenly, we see that something in the middle distance*
*is on fire. The wide dark fields begin to light up.*

*Voices cry alarm. Shouts, cries. Everyone and every-
thing is lit by the shaking radiance of the fire.*

VACARRO *races towards the fire. It is in the gin building. The volatile dust explodes. Loaded wagons are
being pushed away, by Negro field hands driven by*
VACARRO.

*A fire engine arrives. But it seems lax in its efforts and
inefficient. A hose is pulled out, but there is insufficient
water to play water on the blaze, and the hose itself
falls short. The firemen are not merely ineffectual.
Some seem actually indifferent. In fact, some of their
faces express an odd pleasure in the flames, which they
seem more interested in watching than fighting.*

VACARRO *rushes among them exhorting, commanding,
constantly gesturing with his short riding crop. In his
frenzy, he lashes the crop at the man holding the fire
hose. The man, resentfully, throws the end of the hose
at* VACARRO, *who seizes the nozzle and walks directly
towards and into the flames.*

*Now men try to stop him.* VACARRO *turns the hose on
them, driving them back and then goes into the flames.
He disappears from sight. All we hear is his shouts in
a foreign tongue.*

*A wall collapses.*

*The hose suddenly leaps about as if it has been freed.
The crowd. Horrified. Then they see something. . . .*

VACARRO *comes out. He holds aloft a small, gallon-size
kerosene can. He strikes at his trouser bottoms, which
are hot. He is on the point of collapse. Men rush to
him and drag him to a safe distance. He clutches the
can.*

*They lay him out, and crouch around him. He is*
*smudged and singed. His eyes open, look around.*
*His viewpoint. From this distorted angle, lit by the vic-*
*torious flames are a circle of faces which are either*
*indifferent or downright unfriendly. Some cannot con-*
*trol a faint smile.*
VACARRO *clutches the can, closes his eyes.*
*Another wall collapses.*

DISSOLVE.

31]

EXTERIOR. ARCHIE LEE'S HOUSE. NIGHT.
ARCHIE LEE's *car turns into the drive. He descends*
*noiselessly as a thief. Camera follows him, and it and*
*he discover* BABY DOLL *on the porch swing. There are*
*several suitcases, packed and ready to go. In a chair near*
*the porch swing, sleeping as mildly as a baby, is* AUNT
ROSE COMFORT.

ARCHIE:

What are doin' out here at one o'clock in the morning?

BABY DOLL:

I'm not talking to you.

ARCHIE:

What are you doing out here?

BABY DOLL:

Because in the first place, I didn't have the money to
pay for a hotel room, because you don't give me any
money, because you don't have any money, and sec-
ondly, because if I had the money I couldn't have no
way of getting there because you went off in the Chevy,

and leave me no way of getting anywhere, including to the fire which I wanted to see just like everyone else.

ARCHIE:

What fire you talking about?

BABY DOLL:

What fire am I talking about?

ARCHIE:

I don't know about no fire.

BABY DOLL:

You must be crazy or think I'm crazy. You mean to tell me you don't know the cotton gin burned down at the Syndicate Plantation right after you left the house.

ARCHIE:

*(Seizing her arm)*

Hush up. I never left this house.

BABY DOLL:

You certainly did leave this house. OW!!

ARCHIE:

Look here! Listen to what I tell you. I never left this house. . . .

BABY DOLL:

You certainly did and left me here without a coke in the place. OWW!! Cut it out!!

ARCHIE:

Listen to what I tell you. I went up to bed with my bottle after supper——

BABY DOLL:

What bed! OW!

ARCHIE:

And passed out dead to the world. You got that in your

haid?? Will you remember that now?

BABY DOLL:

Let' go my arm!

ARCHIE:

What did I do after supper?

BABY DOLL:

You know what you did, you jumped in the Chevy an' disappeared after supper and didn't get back till just —— OWWW!!! Will you quit twisting my arm.

ARCHIE:

I'm trying to wake you up. You're asleep, you're dreaming! What did I do after supper?

BABY DOLL:

Went to bed! Leggo! Went to bed. Leggo! Leggo!

ARCHIE:

That's right. Make sure you remember. I went to bed after supper and didn't wake up until I heard the fire whistle blow and I was too drunk to git up and drive the car. Now come inside and go to bed.

BABY DOLL:

Go to what bed? I got no bed to go to!

ARCHIE:

You will tomorrow. The furniture is coming back tomorrow.

BABY DOLL *whimpers.*

ARCHIE:

(*Continues*)

Did I hurt my little baby's arm?

BABY DOLL:

Yais.

ARCHIE:

Where I hurt little baby's arm?

BABY DOLL:

Here. . . .

ARCHIE:

(*He puts a big wet kiss on her arm*)
Feel better?

BABY DOLL:

No. . . .

ARCHIE:

(*Another kiss. This travels up her arm*)
My sweet baby doll. My sweet little baby doll.

BABY DOLL:

(*Sleepily*)
Hurt. . . . MMMmmmmm! Hurt.

ARCHIE:

Hurt?

BABY DOLL:

Mmm!

ARCHIE:

Kiss?

BABY DOLL:

Mmmmmmmmm.

ARCHIE:

Baby sleepy?

BABY DOLL:

MMmmmmm.

ARCHIE:

Kiss good. . . ?

BABY DOLL:

Mmmmm. . . .

ARCHIE:

Make little room . . . good. . . .

BABY DOLL:

Too hot.

ARCHIE:

Make a little room, go on. . . .

BABY DOLL:

Mmmm. . . .

ARCHIE:

Whose baby? Big sweet . . . whose baby?

BABY DOLL:

You hurt me. . . . Mmmm. . . .

ARCHIE:

Kiss. . . .

*He lifts her wrist to his lips and makes gobbling sound.
We get an idea of what their courtship—such as it was
—was like. Also how passionately he craves her, willing
to take her under any conditions, including fast asleep.*

BABY DOLL:

Stop it. . . . Silly. . . . Mmmmmm. . . .

ARCHIE:

What would I do if you was a big piece of cake?

BABY DOLL:

Silly.

ARCHIE:

Gobble! Gobble!

BABY DOLL:

Oh you. . . .

ARCHIE:

What would I do if you was angel food cake? Big
white piece with lots of nice thick icin'?

BABY DOLL:

    (*Giggling now, in spite of herself. She's also sleepy*)

    Quit.

ARCHIE:

    (*As close as he's ever been to having her*)

    Gobble! Gobble! Gobble!

BABY DOLL:

    Archie!

ARCHIE:

    Hmmmmm. . . .

    (*He's working on her arm*)

    Skrunch, gobble, ghrumpt . . . etc.

BABY DOLL:

    You tickle. . . .

ARCHIE:

    Answer little question. . . .

BABY DOLL:

    What?

ARCHIE:

    (*Into her arm*)

    Where I been since supper?

BABY DOLL:

    Off in the Chevy——

    *Instantly he seizes her wrist again. She shrieks. The romance is over.*

ARCHIE:

    Where I been since supper?

BABY DOLL:

    Upstairs. . . .

ARCHIE:

    Doing what?

BABY DOLL:

With your bottle. Archie, leggo. . . .

ARCHIE:

And what else. . . .

BABY DOLL:

Asleep. Leggo. . . .

ARCHIE:

(*Letting go*)

Now you know where I been and what I been doing since supper. In case anybody asks.

BABY DOLL:

Yeah.

ARCHIE:

Now go to sleep. . . .

*He seizes her suitcases and goes off into the house. BABY DOLL follows, and AUNT ROSE follows her, asleep on her feet. As they go in, ARCHIE LEE comes out and looks around. Then he listens.*

ARCHIE:

Nice quiet night. Real nice and quiet.

*The gin can no longer be heard.*

CUT TO

32]

BRITE SPOT CAFE. EXTERIOR. NIGHT.

*It's not quiet here at all. The area in front of the entrance is crowded with cars. A holiday mood prevails. It's as if the fire has satisfied some profound and basic hunger and left the people of that community exhilarated.*

*The pickup truck of* SILVA VACARRO *drives up, shoots into a vacant spot. He leaps from the driver's cab. He has not yet washed, his shirt is torn and blackened and he has a crude bandage around the arm that holds the whip. He stands for a few moments beside his truck, looking around at the cars, trying to find the car of the* MARSHAL, *which would indicate that that county official is inside. Then he sees what he's looking for. He walks over to the car which has the official seal on its side, and not finding the* MARSHAL *there, turns and strides into the . . .*

33]

INTERIOR. BRITE SPOT. (A JUKE JOINT)
*Everybody is talking about the fire. The juke box is a loud one. There are some dancing couples.*

SILVA VACARRO *passes by a little knot of men. He is followed by* ROCK, *holding the kerosene can. The Camera stays with them. They smile.*

A MAN:

That ole boy is really burning!
*One of the men detaches himself and moves in the direction that* VACARRO *took. Then another follows.*

34]

GROUP OF MEN AROUND THE MARSHAL.

MARSHAL:

What makes you think your gin was set fire to?

SILVA:

Look around you. Did you ever see such a crowd of happy faces, looks like a rich man's funeral with all his relations attending.

MARSHAL:

I'd hate to have to prove it.

SILVA:

I'd hate to have to depend on you to prove it.

*The man from the other group walks up.*

MAN:

What are you going to do about ginning out your cotton?

SILVA:

I'll truck it over to Sunset. Collins'll gin it out for me.

MAN:

Collins got cotton of his own to gin.

SILVA:

Then I'll truck it across the river. Ain't nobody around here's gonna gin it.

MAN:

I'm all set up to do it for you.

SILVA:

I wouldn't give you the satisfaction.

*The men drift back a few steps.*

MARSHAL:

(*He speaks a little for the benefit of the men in the room*)

I honestly can't imagine if it was a case of arson who could of done it since every man jack that you put out of business was standing right there next to the platform when the fire broke out.

ROCK:

One wasn't. I know one that wasn't.

MARSHAL:

(*Wheeling on bar stool to face him. Sharply*)
Looky here, boy! Naming names is risky, just on suspicion.

ROCK:

I didn't name his name. I just said I know it. And the initials are stamped on this here can.

MARSHAL:

(*Quickly*)
Let's break it up, break it up, not the time or the place to make accusations, I'll take charge of this can. I'll examine it carefully to see if there's any basis for thinking it was used to start a fire with.

SILVA:

(*Cutting in*)
I run through fire to git that can, and I mean to keep it.
(*Then to* ROCK)
Lock it up in the pickup truck.

ROCK *leaves. Unobtrusively some men follow him.*

MARSHAL:

Vacarro. Come over here. I want to have a word with you in one of these booths. . . .

35]

ROCK.

*He enters the men's room. As he approaches the urinal, the light is switched out and the door is thown open at the same moment. Hoarse muffled shouts and sounds of struggle and a metallic clatter. Then the light goes on and* ROCK *is lying on the filthy cement floor, dazed.* VACARRO *enters. He goes to* ROCK.

ROCK:

They got the can, boss.

SILVA:

Whose initials was on it? Huh? You said you seen some initials on the can.

ROCK:

Naw. It just said—Sears and Roebuck.

*The* MARSHAL *has come in and now reaches down and helps* ROCK *to regain his feet. . . .*

MARSHAL:

Sears and Roebuck! That does it! Hahaha. Boy, git up and git some black coffee in yuh.

*They pass through the door.*

36]

THE MAIN ROOM.

MARSHAL:

Ruby, Ruby! Give this boy some black coffee. He had a bad fall in the outhouse. Hawhawhaw. . . .

*But* SILVA *has steered* ROCK *out the front door and they are gone. The* MARSHAL *follows . . .*

37]

OUTSIDE.

SILVA *and* ROCK *head towards the pickup. The* MARSHAL *appears in the doorway.*

MARSHAL:

Vacarro!

Silva *and* Rock *are at the truck. They wait for the* Marshal, *who is walking towards them.*

MARSHAL:

(*Soberly, plainly*)

You take the advice of an old man who knows this county like the back of his hand. It's true you made a lot of enemies here. You happen to be a man with foreign blood. That's a disadvantage in this county. A disadvantage at least to begin with. But you added stubbornness and suspicion and resentment.

Vacarro *makes an indescribable sound.*

MARSHAL:

I still say, a warm, friendly attitude on your part could have overcome that quickly. Instead, you stood off from people, refused to fraternize with them. Why not drop that attitude now? If some one set fire to your gin—I say that's not impossible. Also, I say we'll find him. But I don't have to tell you that if you now take your cotton across the river, or into another county, it will give rise to a lot of unfriendly speculation. No one would like it. No one.

*Abruptly he turns and goes.*

Rock *and* Silva *are left alone. Men watch them from the surrounding cars . . . from the doorway.*

SILVA:

Did you ever see so many happy faces? Which one did it, Rock, you said you knew. . . ?

ROCK:

Well, they're all here . . . all here except one. The one that ain't here, I figure he did it. . . .

*They're getting into the pickup.*

SILVA:

Well, he's the one that's gonna gin out my cotton. . . .
*The motor starts . . . the car goes into gear . . . and
moves.*

DISSOLVE.

38]

THE ROAD BEFORE ARCHIE LEE'S HOUSE.
THE NEXT MORNING.

SILVA's *pickup truck is leading a long line of cotton
wagons—full of cotton.*

39]

CLOSER SHOT. THE PICKUP.

*It stops.*

40]

CLOSE ANGLE. SILVA AND ROCK.

ROCK:

Maybe it figures. But it sure puzzles me why you want
to bring your cotton to the guy that burned down your
gin. . . .

SILVA:

You don't know the Christian proverbs about how you
turn the other cheek when one has been slapped. . . .

ROCK:

When both cheeks has been kicked, what are you
gonna turn then?

SILVA:

You just got to turn and keep turning. Stop the wagons!

I'm gonna drive up to his house.

Rock *hops out of the pickup truck.*

41]

OUTSIDE MEIGHAN HOUSE.

*At an upstairs window we can just see* Archie's *face. He is watching the wagons. Suddenly, he withdraws his head.*

42]

UPSTAIRS. ARCHIE LEE MEIGHAN'S HOUSE.

*He goes into a crazy, but silent Indian war dance. Then suddenly he can no longer contain himself and runs into . . .*

43]

THE NURSERY.

*Enter* Archie Lee.

Baby Doll *is asleep in the crib. Her thumb is in her mouth. Like a child, she's trying to hold on to her sleep.* Archie Lee *just whoops and hollers.* "Baby Doll! Baby Doll!!", *etc.* "Get up . . ." *etc.*

*She can hardly believe her eyes. . . .*

*From downstairs the pickup's horn sounds urgently.*

Aunt Rose Comfort *rushes in breathlessly . . .*

AUNT ROSE:

Archie Lee, honesy. . . .

ARCHIE:

(*Very Big Shot*)

Get her up! Get her up, get her washed and dressed and

*Page 47*

looking decent. Then bring her down. The furniture is
coming back today. . . .
*He exits . . .*

44]/65]

FRONT YARD.

SILVA *and* ROCK *are sitting there in the pickup truck.
They sit a little formally and stiffly and wait for*
MEIGHAN, *who comes barreling out of the house, and up
to the pickup.*

ARCHIE:

Don't say a word. A little bird already told me that
you'd be bringing those twenty-seven wagons full of
cotton straight to my door, and I want you to know
that you're a very lucky fellow.

ROCK:

(*Dryly*)

How come?

ARCHIE:

I mean that I am in a position to hold back other orders
and give you a priority. Well! Come on out of that
truck and have some coffee.

SILVA:

What's your price?

ARCHIE:

You remember my price. It hasn't changed.

*Silence. The sense that* SILVA *is inspecting him.*

ARCHIE:

Hey, now looka here. Like you take shirts to a laundry.
You take them Friday and you want them Saturday.
That's special. You got to pay special.

SILVA:

How about your equipment? Hasn't changed either?

ARCHIE:

A-1 shape! Always was! You ought to remember.

SILVA:

I remember you needed a new saw-cylinder. You got one?

ARCHIE:

Can't find one on the market to equal the old one yet. Come on down and have a cup of coffee. We're all ready for you.

SILVA:

I guess when you saw my gin burning down last night you must've suspected that you might get a good deal of business thrown your way in the morning.

ARCHIE:

You want to know something?

SILVA:

I'm always glad to know something when there's something to know.

ROCK *laughs wildly.*

ARCHIE:

I never seen that fire of yours last night! Now come on over to my house and have some coffee.

*The men get out of the truck.* ARCHIE *speaks to* ROCK.

ARCHIE:

You come too, if you want to. . . . No, sir, I never seen that fire of yours last night. We hit the sack right after supper and didn't know until breakfast time this morning that your cotton gin had burned down.

*They go up on the porch.*

Yes sir, it's providential. That's the only word for it. Hey, Baby Doll! It's downright providential. Baby Doll! Come out here, Baby Doll!

*Enter* BABY DOLL.

You come right over here and meet Mr. Vacarro from the Syndicate Plantation.

BABY DOLL:

Oh hello. Has something gone wrong, Archie Lee?

ARCHIE:

What do you mean, Baby Doll?

BABY DOLL:

I just thought that maybe something went——

ARCHIE:

What is your first name, Vacarro?

SILVA:

Silva.

ARCHIE:

How do you spell it?

SILVA *spells it.* "*Capital S-I-L-V-A.*" *Meantime, his eyes are on* BABY DOLL.

ARCHIE:

Oh. Like a silver lining? Every cloud has got a silver lining.

BABY DOLL:

What is that from? The Bible?

SILVA:

No, the Mother Goose book.

BABY DOLL:

That name sounds foreign.

SILVA:

It is, Mrs. Meighan. I'm known as the wop that runs

the Syndicate Plantation.

ARCHIE LEE *claps him heartily on the back.* SILVA *stiffly withdraws from the contact.*

ARCHIE:

Don't call yourself names. Let other folks call you names! Well, you're a lucky little fellow, silver, gold, or even nickel-plated, you sure are lucky that I can take a job of this size right now. It means some cancellations, but you're my closest neighbor. I believe in the good neighbor policy, Mr. Vacarro. You do me a good turn and I'll do you a good turn. Tit for tat. Tat for tit is the policy we live on. *Aunt Rose Comfort!* Baby Doll, git your daddy's ole maid sister to break out a fresh pot of coffee for Mr. Vacarro.

BABY DOLL:

You get her.

ARCHIE:

And honey, I want you to entertain this gentleman. Ha! Ha! Look at her blush. Haha! This is my baby. This is my little girl, every precious ounce of her is mine, all mine.

*He exits—crazily elated, calling "Aunt Rose."*

*CUT BACK to* BABY DOLL. *She emits an enormous yawn.*

BABY DOLL:

Excuse my yawn. We went to bed kinda late last night.

*CUT TO SILVA. He notices the discrepancy. He looks at* ROCK, *who also noticed.*

*As if she were talking of a title of great distinction.*

So. You're a wop?

SILVA:

(*With ironic politeness*)

I'm a Sicilian, Mrs. Meighan. A very ancient people. . . .

BABY DOLL:

(*Trying out the word*)

Sish! Sish!

SILVA:

No ma'am. Siss! Sicilian.

BABY DOLL:

Oh, how unusual.

ARCHIE LEE *bursts back out on the porch.*

ARCHIE:

And honey, at noon, take Mr. Vacarro in town to the Kotton King Hotel for a chicken dinner. Sign my name! It's only when bad luck hits you, Mr. Vacarro, that you find out who your friends are. I mean to prove it. All right. Let's get GOING! Baby, knock me a kiss!

BABY DOLL:

What's the matter with you? Have you got drunk before breakfast?

ARCHIE:

Hahaha.

BABY DOLL:

Somebody say something funny?

ARCHIE:

Offer this young fellow here to a cup of coffee. I got to get busy ginning that cotton.

*He extends his great sweaty hand to* VACARRO.

Glad to be able to help you out of this bad situation. It's the good neighbor policy.

*Page 52*

SILVA:

What is?

ARCHIE:

You do me a good turn and I'll do you a good turn sometime in the future.

SILVA:

I see.

ARCHIE:

Tit for tat, tat for tit, as they say. Hahaha! Well, make yourself at home here. Baby Doll, I want you to make this gentleman comfortable in the house.

BABY DOLL:

You can't make anyone comfortable in this house. Lucky if you can find a chair to sit in.

*But* MEIGHAN *is gone, calling out: "Move those wagons,"* etc., etc.

BABY DOLL:

(*After a slight pause*)
Want some coffee?

SILVA:

No. Just a cool drink of water, thank you ma'am.

BABY DOLL:

The kitchen water runs warm, but if you got the energy to handle an old-fashioned pump, you can get you a real cool drink from that there cistern at the side of the house. . . .

SILVA:

I got energy to burn.

VACARRO *strides through the tall seeding grass to an old cistern with a hand pump, deep in the side yard.* ROCK *follows.* OLD FUSSY *goes "Squawk, Squawk," and* AUNT

Rose Comfort *is singing "Rock of Ages" in the kitchen.*

SILVA:

(*Looking about contemptuously as he crosses to the cistern*)

Dump their garbage in the yard, phew! *Ignorance* and *Indulgence* and *stink!*

ROCK:

I thought that young Mizz Meighan smelt pretty good.

SILVA:

You keep your nose with the cotton. And hold that dipper, I'll pump.

AUNT ROSE:

Sometimes water comes and sometimes it don't.

*The water comes pouring from the rusty spout.*

SILVA:

This time it did. . . .

BABY DOLL:

Bring me a dipper of that nice cool well water, please.

Rock *crosses immediately with the filled dipper.*

SILVA:

Hey!

OLD FUSSY:

Squawk, squawk!!

AUNT ROSE:

I don't have the strength anymore in my arm that I used to, to draw water out of that pump.

*She approaches, smoothing her ancient apron.* Vacarro *is touched by her aged grace.*

SILVA:

Would you care for a drink?

*Page 54*

AUNT ROSE:

How do you do? I'm Aunt Rose Comfort McCorkle. My brother was Baby Doll's daddy, Mr. T. C. Carson. I've been visiting here since ... since....

*She knits her ancient brow, unable to recall precisely when the long visit started.*

SILVA:

I hope you don't mind drinking out of a gourd.

*He hands her the gourd of well water.* ROCK *returns, saying aloud ...*

ROCK:

I could think of worse ways to spend a hot afternoon than delivering cool well water to Mrs. Meighan.

AUNT ROSE:

SCUSE ME PLEASE! That ole hen, Fussy, has just gone back in my kitchen!

*She runs crazily to the house.* BABY DOLL *has wandered back to the cistern as if unconsciously drawn by the magnetism of the two young males.*

BABY DOLL:

They's such a difference in water! You wouldn't think so, but there certainly is.

SILVA:

(*To* ROCK)
Hold the dipper, I'll pump!

*He brings up more water; then strips off his shirt and empties the brimming dipper over his head and at the same time he says to* ROCK ...

SILVA:

Go stay with the cotton. Go on! Stay with the cotton.

ROCK *goes.*

BABY DOLL:

I wouldn't dare to expose myself like that. I take such terrible sunburn.

SILVA:

I like the feel of a hot sun on my body.

BABY DOLL:

That's not sunburn though. You're natcherally dark.

SILVA:

Yes. Don't you have garbage collectors on Tiger Tail Road?

BABY DOLL:

It cost a little bit extra to git them to come out here and Archie Lee Meighan claimed it was highway robbery! Refused to pay! Now the place is swarming with flies an' mosquitoes and—oh, I don't know, I almost give up sometimes.

SILVA:

And did I understand you to say that you've got a bunch of unfurnished rooms in the house?

BABY DOLL:

Five complete sets of furniture hauled away! By the Ideal Pay As You Go Plan Furniture Company.

SILVA:

When did this misfortune—fall upon you?

BABY DOLL:

Why yestiddy! Ain't that awful?

SILVA:

Both of us had misfortunes on the same day.

BABY DOLL:

Huh?

*Page 56*

SILVA:

You lost your furniture. My cotton gin burned down.

BABY DOLL:

(*Not quite with it*)

Oh.

SILVA:

Quite a coincidence!

BABY DOLL:

Huh?

SILVA:

I said it was a coincidence of misfortune.

BABY DOLL:

Well, sure—after all what can you do with a bunch of unfurnished rooms.

SILVA:

Well, you could play hide-and-seek.

BABY DOLL:

Not me. I'm not athletic.

SILVA:

I take it you've not had this place long, Mrs. Meighan.

BABY DOLL:

No, we ain't had it long.

SILVA:

When I arrived in this county to take over the management of the Syndicate Plantation . . .

(*Chops at grass with crop*)

this place was empty. I was told it was haunted. Then you all moved in.

BABY DOLL:

Yes it was haunted, and that's why Archie Lee bought it for almost nothing.

(*She pauses in the sun as if dazed*)

Sometimes I don't know where to go, what to do.

SILVA:

That's not uncommon. People enter this world without instruction.

BABY DOLL:

(*She's lost him again*)

Huh?

SILVA:

I said people come into this world without instructions of where to go, what to do, so they wander a little and . . .

AUNT ROSE *sings rather sweetly from the kitchen, wind blows an Aeolian refrain.*

then go away. . . .

*Now* BABY DOLL *gives him a quick look, almost perceptive and then* . . .

BABY DOLL:

Yah, well . . .

SILVA:

*Drift*—for a while and then . . . *vanish.*

(*He stoops to pick a dandelion*)

And so make room for newcomers! Old goers, new comers! Back and forth, going and coming, rush, rush!! *Permanent? Nothing!*

(*Blows on the seeding dandelion*)

Anything living! . . . last long enough to take it serious.

*They are walking together. There is the beginning of some weird understanding between them.*

*They have stopped strolling by a poetic wheelless chassis of an old Pierce-Arrow limousine in the side yard.*

Page 58

BABY DOLL:

This is the old Pierce-Arrow car that belonged to the lady that used to own this place and haunts it now.

VACARRO *steps gravely forward and opens the back door for her.*

SILVA:

Where to, madam?

BABY DOLL:

Oh, you're playing *show-fer!* It's a good place to sit when the house isn't furnished. . . .

*She enters and sinks on the ruptured upholstery. He gravely puts the remnant of the dandelion in the cone-shaped cut-glass vase in a bracket by the back seat of the old limousine.*

BABY DOLL:

*(Laughing with sudden, childish laughter)*

Drive me along the river as fast as you can with all the windows open to cool me off.

SILVA:

Fine, Madam!

BABY DOLL:

*(Suddenly aware of his body near her)*

Showfers sit in the front seat.

SILVA:

Front seat's got no cushion.

BABY DOLL:

It's hard to find a place to sit around here since the Ideal Pay As You Go Plan people lost patience. To sit in comfort, I mean. . . .

SILVA:

It's hard to sit in comfort when the Ideal Pay As You

Go Plan people lose their patience and your gin burns down.

BABY DOLL:

Oh! But . . .

SILVA:

Huh?

BABY DOLL:

You said that like you thought there was . . .

SILVA:

What?

BABY DOLL:

Some connection! Excuse me, I want to get out and I can't get over your legs. . . .

*Her apathy is visited by a sudden inexplicable flurry of panic. He has his boots propped against the back of the front seat.*

SILVA:

You can't get over my legs?

BABY DOLL:

No. I'm not athletic.

*She tries to open door on other side, but it is blocked by the trunk of a pecan tree.*

SILVA:

But it's cool here and comfortable to sit in. What's this here??

*He has seized her wrist on which hangs a bracelet of many little gold charms. She sinks somewhat uneasily in beside him.*

BABY DOLL:

It's a, it's a . . . charm bracelet.

*Page 60*

*He begins to finger the many little gold charms attached.*

BABY DOLL:

My daddy gave it to me. Them there's the ten commandments.

SILVA:

And these?

BABY DOLL:

My birthdays. It's stretchable. One for each birthday.

SILVA:

How many charming birthdays have you had?

BABY DOLL:

As many as I got charms hanging on that bracelet.

SILVA:

Mind if I count 'em?

*They are close.*

Fourteen, fifteen, sixteen, seventeen, eighteen, nineteen, and . . .

BABY DOLL:

That's all. I'll be twenty tomorrow. Tomorrow is Election Day and Election Day is my birthday. I was born on the day that Frank Delano Roosevelt was elected for his first term.

SILVA:

A great day for the country for both reasons.

BABY DOLL:

He was a man to respect.

SILVA:

And you're a lady to respect, Mrs. Meighan.

BABY DOLL:

*(Sadly and rather touchingly)*

Me? Oh, no—I never got past the fourth grade.

SILVA:

Why'd you quit?

BABY DOLL:

I had a great deal of trouble with long division. . . .

SILVA:

Yeah?

BABY DOLL:

The teacher would tell me to go to the blackboard and
work out a problem in long division and I would go
to the blackboard and lean my head against it and cry
and cry and—cry. . . .

Whew! I think the porch would be cooler. Mr. Vacarro, I can't get over your legs.

SILVA:

You want to move my legs.

BABY DOLL:

Yes, otherwise, I can't get out of the car. . . .

SILVA:

Okay.

*He raises his legs so she can get out. Which she does,
and continues . . .*

BABY DOLL:

YES, I would cry and cry. . . . Well . . . soon after that
I left school. A girl without education is—without education. . . .

Whew. . . . Feel kind of dizzy. Hope I'm not gettin' a
*sun* stroke. —I better sit in the shade. . . .

VACARRO *follows her casually into the shade of the pecan
tree where there's a decrepit old swing. Suddenly, he
leaps into branches and then down with a pecan. He*

*cracks it in his mouth and hands her the kernels. . . .*

BABY DOLL:

Mr. Vacarro! I wouldn't dream!—excuse me, but I just wouldn't dream! of eating a nut that a man had cracked in his mouth. . . .

SILVA:

You've got many refinements. I don't think you need to worry about your failure at long division. I mean, after all, you got through short division, and short division is all that a lady ought to be called on to cope with. . . .

BABY DOLL:

Well, I—ought to go in, but I get depressed when I pass through those empty rooms. . . .

SILVA:

All the rooms empty?

BABY DOLL:

All but the nursery. And the kitchen. The stuff in those rooms was paid for. . . .

SILVA:

You have a child in the nursery?

BABY DOLL:

Me? No. I sleep in the nursery myself. Let down the slats on the crib. . . .

SILVA:

Why do you sleep in the nursery?

BABY DOLL:

Mr. Vacarro, that's a *personal* question.

*There is a pause.*

BABY DOLL:

I ought to go in . . . but . . . you know there are places

in that house which I never been in. I mean the attic
for instance. Most of the time I'm afraid to go into that
house by myself. Last night when the fire broke out I
sat here on this swing for hours and hours till Archie
Lee got home, because I was scared to enter this old
place by myself.

VACARRO *has caught this discrepancy too.*

SILVA:

It musta been scary here without your husband to look
after you.

BABY DOLL:

I'm tellin' you! The fire lit up the whole countryside
and it made big crazy shadows and we didn't have a
coke in the house and the heat and the mosquitoes and
—I was mad at Archie Lee.

SILVA:

Mad at Mr. Meighan? What about?

BABY DOLL:

Oh, he went off and left me settin' here without a coke
in the place.

SILVA:

Went off and left you, did he??!!

BABY DOLL:

Well, he certainly did. Right after supper and when he
got back, the fire'd already broke out. I got smoke in
my eyes and my nose and throat. I was in such a worn-
out nervous condition it made me cry. Finally I took
two teaspoons of paregoric.

SILVA:

Sounds like you passed a very uncomfortable night.

BABY DOLL:

Sounds like? Well it was!

SILVA:

So Mr. Meighan—you say—disappeared after supper.

BABY DOLL:

*(After a pause)*
Huh?

SILVA:

You say Mr. Meighan left the house for a while after supper?

*Something in his tone makes her aware that she has spoken indiscreetly.*

BABY DOLL:

Oh—uh—just for a moment.

SILVA:

Just for a moment, huh? How long a moment?

BABY DOLL:

What are you driving at, Mr. Vacarro?

SILVA:

Driving at? Nothing.

BABY DOLL:

You're looking at me so funny.

SILVA:

How long a moment did he disappear for? Can you remember, Mrs. Meighan?

BABY DOLL:

What difference does that make? What's it to you, anyhow?

SILVA:

Why should you mind my asking?

BABY DOLL:

You make this sound like I was on trial for something.

SILVA:

Don't you like to pretend like you're a witness?

BABY DOLL:

Witness of what, Mr. Vacarro?

SILVA:

Why—for instance—say—a case of arson!

BABY DOLL:

Case of——? What is—arson?

SILVA:

The willful destruction of property by fire.

*(Slaps his boots sharply with the riding crop)*

BABY DOLL:

Oh!

*(She nervously fingers her purse)*

SILVA:

There's one thing I always notice about you ladies.

BABY DOLL:

What's that?

SILVA:

Whenever you get nervous, you always like to have something in your hands to hold on to—like that big white purse.

BABY DOLL:

This purse?

SILVA:

Yes, it gives you something to hold on to, isn't that right?

BABY DOLL:

Well, I do always like to have something in my hands.

*Page 66*

SILVA:

Sure you do. You feel what a lot of uncertain things there are. Gins burn down. No one know how or why. Volunteer fire departments don't have decent equipment. They're no protection. The afternoon sun is too hot. The trees! They're no protection! The house—it's haunted! It's no protection. Your husband. He's across the road and busy. He's no protection! The goods that dress is made of—it's light and thin—it's no protection. So what do you do, Mrs. Meighan? You pick up that white kid purse. It's something to hold on to.

BABY DOLL:

Now, Mr. Silva. Don't you go and be getting any— funny ideas.

SILVA:

Ideas about what?

BABY DOLL:

My husband disappearing—after supper. I can explain that.

SILVA:

Can you?

BABY DOLL:

Sure I can.

SILVA:

Good! How do you explain it?
*(He stares at her. She looks down)*
What's the matter? Can't you collect your thoughts, Mrs. Meighan?
*(Pause)*
Your mind's a blank on the subject??

BABY DOLL:

Look here, now. . . .

SILVA:

You find it impossible to remember just what your husband disappeared for after supper? You can't imagine what kind of an errand he went out on, can you?

BABY DOLL:

No! No! I can't!

SILVA:

But when he returned—let's see—the fire had just broken out at the Syndicate Plantation.

BABY DOLL:

Mr. Vacarro, I don't have the slightest idea what you could be driving at.

SILVA:

You're a very unsatisfactory witness, Mrs. Meighan.

BABY DOLL:

I never can think when people—stare straight at me.

SILVA:

Okay, I'll look away then.

*(Turns his back to her)*

Now, does that improve your memory any? Now are you able to concentrate on the question?

BABY DOLL:

Huh?

SILVA:

No? You're not?

*(Grins evilly)* .

Well—should we drop the subject??

BABY DOLL:

I sure do wish you would!

SILVA:

Sure, there's no use crying over a burnt-down gin. And besides, like your husband says—this world is built on the principle of tit for tat.

BABY DOLL:

What do you mean?

SILVA:

Nothing at all specific. Mind if I . . . ?

BABY DOLL:

What?

SILVA *approaches the swing where she sits.*

SILVA:

You want to move over a little and make some room?

BABY DOLL:

*(Shifts slightly)*

Is that room enough for you?

SILVA:

Enough for me. How about you?

BABY DOLL:

Is it strong enough to support us both?

SILVA:

I hope. Let's swing a little. You seem all tense. Motion relaxes people. It's like a cradle. A cradle relaxes a baby. They call you "Baby," don't they?

BABY DOLL:

That's sort of a pet name.

SILVA:

Well in the swing you can relax like a cradle. . . .

BABY DOLL:

Not if you swing it so high. It shakes me up.

SILVA:

Well, I'll swing it low then. Are you relaxed?

BABY DOLL:

I'm relaxed enough. As much as necessary.

SILVA:

No, you're not. Your nerves are all tied up.

BABY DOLL:

You make me nervous.

SILVA:

Just swinging with you?

BABY DOLL:

Not just that.

SILVA:

What else then?

BABY DOLL:

All them questions you asked me about the fire.

SILVA:

I only inquired about your husband—about his leaving the house after supper.

BABY DOLL:

Why should I have to explain why he left the house? Besides, I did. I think I explained that to you.

SILVA:

You said that he left the house before the fire broke out.

BABY DOLL:

What about it?

SILVA:

Why did he leave the house?

BABY DOLL:

I explained that to you. I explained that to you.

SILVA:

What was the explanation? I forgot it.

*Baby Doll's face is beaded with sweat. To save her life she can't think, can't think at all.*

BABY DOLL:

*(Just to gain a moment)*

Oh, you're talking about my husband?

SILVA:

That's who I'm talking about.

BABY DOLL:

How should I know!!!

SILVA:

You mean where he went after supper.

BABY DOLL:

Yes!! How should I know where he went.

SILVA:

I thought you said you explained that to me.

BABY DOLL:

I did! I explained it to you!

SILVA:

Well, if you don't know, how could you explain it to me?

BABY DOLL:

*(Turning)*

There's no reason why I should explain things to you.

SILVA:

Then just relax.

*They swing.*

As I was saying, that was a lovely remark your husband made.

BABY DOLL:

What remark did he make?

SILVA:

The good neighbor policy. I see what he means by that now.

BABY DOLL:

He was talking about the President's speech.

SILVA:

I think he was talking about something closer to home. *You do me* a good turn and *I'll do you* one. That was the way he put it.

*Delicately he removes a little piece of lint from her arm.*

SILVA:

There now!

BABY DOLL:

*(Nervously)*

Thanks.

SILVA:

There's a lot of fine cotton lint floating around in the air.

BABY DOLL:

I know there is. It irritates my sinus.

SILVA:

Well, you're a delicate woman.

BABY DOLL:

Delicate? Me? Oh no. I'm a good-size woman.

SILVA:

There's a lot of you, but every bit of you is delicate. Choice. Delectable, I might say.

BABY DOLL:

Huh?

SILVA:

*(Running his finger lightly over her skin)*
You're fine fibered. And smooth. And soft.

BABY DOLL:

Our conversation is certainly taking a personal turn!

SILVA:

Yes! You make me think of cotton.
*(Still caressing her arm another moment)*
No! No fabric, no kind of cloth, not even satin or silk cloth, or no kind of fiber, not even cotton fiber has the ab-so-lute delicacy of your skin!

BABY DOLL:

Well! Should I say thanks or something?

SILVA:

No, just smile, Mrs. Meighan. You have an attractive smile. Dimples!!

BABY DOLL:

No . . .

SILVA:

Yes, you have! Smile, Mrs. Meighan! Come on! Smile!
BABY DOLL *averts her face, smiles helplessly.*
There now. See? You've got them!
*Delicately, he touches one of the indentations in her cheek.*

BABY DOLL:

Please don't touch me. I don't like to be touched.

SILVA:

Then why do you giggle?

BABY DOLL:

Can't help it. You make me feel kind of hysterical, Mr. Vacarro . . . Mr. Vacarro . . .

SILVA:

Yes?

BABY DOLL:

*(A different attack, more feminine, pleading)*
I hope you don't think that Archie Lee was mixed up in that fire. I swear to goodness he never left the front porch. I remember it perfectly now. We just set here on the swing till the fire broke out and then we drove into town.

SILVA:

To celebrate!

BABY DOLL:

No, no, no!

SILVA:

Twenty-seven wagons full of cotton's a pretty big piece of business to fall into your lap like a gift from the gods, Mrs. Meighan.

BABY DOLL:

I thought you said we would drop the subject.

SILVA:

You brought it up that time.

BABY DOLL:

Well, please don't try to mix me up anymore, I swear to goodness the fire had already broke out when he got back.

SILVA:

That's not what you told me a moment ago.

*Page 74*

BABY DOLL:

You got me all twisted up. We went in town. The fire broke out and we didn't know about it.

SILVA:

I thought you said it irritated your sinus.

BABY DOLL:

Oh my God, you sure put words in my mouth. Maybe I'd better make us some lemonade.

*She starts to get up. Silva pulls her down.*

What did you do that for?

SILVA:

I don't want to be deprived of your company yet.

*He lightly switches her legs with his crop.*

BABY DOLL:

(*Twisting*)

Mr. Vacarro, you're getting awfully familiar.

SILVA:

Haven't you got any fun-loving spirit about you?

BABY DOLL:

This isn't fun.

SILVA:

Then why do you giggle?

BABY DOLL:

I'm ticklish!

SILVA:

Ticklish!

BABY DOLL:

Yes, quit switching me, will you?

SILVA:

I'm just shooing the flies off.

BABY DOLL:

They don't hurt nothing. And would you mind moving your arm?

SILVA:

Don't be so skittish!

BABY DOLL:

All right! I'll get up then.

SILVA:

Go on.

BABY DOLL:

*(Trying)*
I feel so weak.
*(She pulls herself away from him)*
Oh! My head's so buzzy.

SILVA:

Fuzzy?

BABY DOLL:

Fuzzy and buzzy. My head's swinging around. It's that swinging. . . . Is something on my arm?

SILVA:

No.

BABY DOLL:

Then what are you brushing?

SILVA:

Sweat off. Let me wipe it. . . .
*He brushes her arm with his handkerchief.*

BABY DOLL:

*(Laughing weakly)*
No, please don't. It feels funny.

Page 76

SILVA:

How does it feel?

BABY DOLL:

Funny! All up and down. You cut it out now. If you don't cut it out I'm going to call.

SILVA:

Call who?

BABY DOLL:

That nigger who's cuttin' the grass across the road.

SILVA:

Go on. Call then.

BABY DOLL:

Hey!

(Her voice is faint, weak)

Hey, boy, boy!

SILVA:

Can't you call any louder?

BABY DOLL:

I feel so funny! What's the matter with me?

SILVA:

You're just relaxing. You're big. There's a lot of you and it's all relaxing! So give in. Stop getting yourself all excited.

BABY DOLL:

I'm not—but you. . . .

SILVA:

I!???

BABY DOLL:

Yes. You. Suspicions. The ideas you have about my husband . . . suspicions.

SILVA:

Suspicions? Such as . . .

BABY DOLL:

Such as he burnt your gin down.

SILVA:

Well?

BABY DOLL:

He didn't.

SILVA:

Didn't he?

BABY DOLL:

I'm going inside. I'm going in the house.

*She starts in. He follows close beside her.*

SILVA:

But you're afraid of the house! Do you believe in ghosts, Mrs. Meighan? I do. I believe in the presence of evil spirits.

BABY DOLL:

What evil spirits you talking about now?

SILVA:

Spirits of violence—and cunning—malevolence—cruelty —treachery—destruction. . . .

BABY DOLL:

Oh, them's just human characteristics.

SILVA:

They're evil spirits that haunt the human heart and take possession of it, and spread from one human heart to another human heart the way that a fire goes springing from leaf to leaf and branch to branch in a tree till a forest is all aflame with it—the birds take flight—the wild things are suffocated . . . everything green and beautiful is destroyed. . . .

BABY DOLL:

You have got fire on the brain.

SILVA:

I see it as more than it seems to be on the surface. I saw it last night as an explosion of those evil spirits that haunt the human heart—I fought it! I ran into it, beating it, stamping it, shouting the curse of God at it! They dragged me out, suffocating. I was defeated! When I came to, lying on the ground—the fire had won the battle, and all around was a ring of human figures! The fire lit their faces! I looked up. And they were illuminated! Their eyes, their teeth were SHINING!! SEE! LIKE THIS!

*He twists his face into a grotesque grimace of pleasure. He holds her. They have arrived at the door to the interior of the house.*

Yeah! Like this! Like this!!

*He thrusts his grimacing face at her. She springs back, frightened.*

BABY DOLL:

Hey! Please! Don't do that! Don't scare me!

SILVA:

The faces I saw—were grinning! Then I knew! I knew the fire was not accidental!

*He holds her fast at the door.*

BABY DOLL:

(*Weakly*)
Not accidental?

SILVA:

No, it was not accidental! It was an expression, a mani-
festation of the human will to *destroy*.

BABY DOLL:

I wouldn't—feel that way—about it. . . .

SILVA:

I do! I do! And so I say I believe in ghosts, in haunted
places, places haunted by the people that occupy them
with hearts overrun by demons of hate and destruction.
I believe his place, this house is haunted. . . . What's
the matter?

BABY DOLL:

*(Now thoroughly shaken)*

I don't know. . . .

SILVA:

You're scared to enter the house, is that the trouble?

BABY DOLL:

*(Calling)*

Aunt Rose. Aunt Rose!!

*(No answer)*

That old woman can't hear a thing.

SILVA:

There's no question about it. This place is haunted.

BABY DOLL:

I'm getting—I'm getting so thirsty, so hot and thirsty!

SILVA:

Then why don't you treat yourself to a drink of cold
water?

BABY DOLL:

I—I thought I might make us a—pitcher of—cold lemonade.

*For some reason,* BABY DOLL *doesn't want to enter the front door and she starts around the porch away from him. A board cracks under her weight. She screams, staggers.* SILVA *rushes to her and seizes her plump arm, placing an arm behind her. She giggles weakly, but for the first time accepting his help.*

BABY DOLL:

The place is—collapsing right underneath me!

SILVA:

You're trembling, Mrs. Meighan, shaking all over!

BABY DOLL:

Your—your hands are so—hot—I don't think I ever felt hands as hot as your hands, they're—why they're like a couple of plates—took right out of—the oven!

SILVA:

Burn, do they?

BABY DOLL:

Yeah, they—*do,* they *burn*—me. . . .

SILVA:

The idea of lemonade is very attractive. I would be glad to help you squeeze the lemons.
*(Tightens the pressure of his hands)*

BABY DOLL:

I know you would! I mean I—thanks, but—I can do it myself.

SILVA:

You don't want my assistance, Mrs. Meighan?

BABY DOLL:

Naw, it ain't necessary. . . .

SILVA:

But then you would have to go into the house alone and the house is haunted! I better go in with you!

BABY DOLL:

. . . No, it ain't necessary!

*(She is panting)*

SILVA:

You want me to stay on the porch?

BABY DOLL:

Yeh, you stay on the porch!

SILVA:

Why *shouldn't* I come inside?

BABY DOLL:

No reason, just—just . . . !

*(She giggles weakly)*

You stay out here while I make the lemonade and . . .

SILVA:

All right. Go on, Mrs. Meighan. . . .

BABY DOLL:

You stay out here. . . .

*He doesn't answer. She stares at him, not moving.*

SILVA:

Now what's the matter now? Why don't you go in?

BABY DOLL:

I don't think I better. I think I will go across the road to the gin. They got a water cooler. . . .

SILVA:

The water cooler's for colored. A lady, a white lady like you, the wife of the big white boss, would place herself in an undignified position if she went over the road to drink with the hands! They might get notions about her! Unwholesome ideas! The sight of her soft white flesh, so smooth and abundant, might inflame their—natures . . .

*Suddenly,* BABY DOLL *sees something off and . . .*

66]

NEGRO BOY COMING DOWN THE ROAD.
*He pushes a lawnmower. Behind him can be seen* ARCHIE LEE's *gin, working.*

67]

BABY DOLL.
*She rushes past* SILVA *in the direction of the Negro boy, runs unsteadily as if she were drunk, across the unkempt lawn and out into the shimmering brilliance of the road.*

BABY DOLL:
Boy! Boy! I want you to cut my grass.

BOY:
Can't now, ma'am.

BABY DOLL:
Yes, you can.

BOY:
I got a job cuttin' grass across Tiger Tail Bayou.

BABY DOLL:
You cut grass here.
*Her intensity frightens the boy.*

BOY:
Yes, ma'am, later.

BABY DOLL:

NO! NOW! RIGHT NOW! I—I'll pay you five dollars. . . .

BOY:

Yes, ma'am.

BABY DOLL:

I'll pay you five dollars . . . but *now*.

BOY:

*(Scared to death)*

Yes ma'am. Yes ma'am.

BABY DOLL:

And work close to the house. Hear! Speak up. Do you hear. . . ?

BOY:

Yes ma'am. Yes ma'am.

BABY DOLL *sees* . . .


68]

SILVA.

*As he comes into the picture, she retreats, walking backwards. Then there is a hoot from the gin. The sound from the gin suddenly stops. This calls her attention to the gin and she starts in that direction.*

SILVA:

Boy.

BOY:

Yes, sir.

SILVA:

Here's that five dollars the lady was mentioning.

*Page 84*

BOY:

   Yes, sir.

SILVA:

   Only she don't want you to cut the grass.

BOY:

   Yes, sir.

SILVA:

   So you go on like you were. Understand?

BOY:

   Oh, yes, sir. Thank you, sir.

   *The boy, now completely bewildered, goes on, as he was.*

69]

INTERIOR.  COTTON GIN.

   *Something is wrong. The men, including* ROCK, *are gathered around a large piece of machinery. There is the characteristic debate as to what is wrong, opinions differing.*

   *Onto this rather hectic group runs* BABY DOLL. ARCHIE *turns on her viciously.*

ARCHIE:

   What're you doin' here, have you gone crazy??

BABY DOLL:

   I want to tell you something! You big slob.

   *This is just a little more than a desperate and harassed* ARCHIE *can bear. He suddenly comes across and smacks* BABY DOLL. *Good and hard!*

ARCHIE:

   I told you never, never, never, to cross that road to this cotton gin——

70]

CLOSE SHOT. SILVA.
*He has entered and seen the action.*

71]

ARCHIE.
*He notices* SILVA.

ARCHIE:

. . . this cotton gin when niggers are working here.

BABY DOLL:

You left me . . . you know what you left with me over
there. . . .

ARCHIE'*s eye wanders over to* SILVA, *and* BABY DOLL *sees
him and clams up.*

72]

SILVA.
*He now officially enters the scene.*

SILVA:

How's progress, Mr. Meighan?

ARCHIE:

Fine! Great!

SILVA:

Personally, I can't hear the gin at all.

BABY DOLL:

*(Full of disgust)*
Big Shot!
*And she exits.*

SILVA:

What's holding up?

*Page 86*

ARCHIE:

Nothing. . . .

SILVA:

Rock!

*Silva's own foreman steps forward.*

ROCK:

His saw-cylinder is busted.

SILVA:

It figures. I inspected your equipment, Meighan, before I put in my own and I put up my own cotton gin because this equipment was rotten, was rotten, and still is rotten. Now it's quarter past two by my watch and I counted twenty-three fully loaded wagons still out on your runway. And if you can't move those wagons any faster . . .

ARCHIE:

Now don't go into any hysterics. You Italians are prone to get too excited. . . .

SILVA:

Never mind about we Italians. You better get yourself a new saw-cylinder and get this contraption running again. And if you can't get one in Clarksdale, you better go to Tunica, and if you can't get one in Tunica, you better go to Memphis, and if you can't get one in Memphis, keep going to St. Louis. Now get on your horse.

ARCHIE:

Now listen to me, Silva——

SILVA:

One more crack out of you, I'm going to haul across the river. I said get on your horse.

MEIGHAN *hesitates. Then decides he must swallow this humiliation. There's nothing else for him to do under the circumstances. He exits.*
SILVA *calls* ROCK *over close.*

SILVA:

*(Sotto voce)*

I got a saw-cylinder in our commissary. Go get it and bring Hank over to help you put it in. Get this thing running. He ain't gonna get one in Clarksdale and if he goes to Memphis—well, don't wait for him.
*And he exits.*

73]

ARCHIE LEE IN HIS CHEVY.

*He nearly runs* BABY DOLL *over.*

BABY DOLL:

Archie Lee! Archie Lee! Archie Lee!
*She stumbles to her knees. She's sobbing. She rests a moment in the tall grass.*

74]

SILVA.

*He runs up to her and stoops down to help her.*

BABY DOLL:

Le' me go. Le' me go.
*She gets up and moves away from him towards her house.*

*Page 88*

AUNT ROSE COMFORT, AND BABY DOLL.

Aunt Rose *comes out of the house all dressed up.*

BABY DOLL:

Aunt Rose Comfort.

Aunt Rose Comfort *rushes past her.*

BABY DOLL:

Aunt Rose Comfort!! Where are you going?

AUNT ROSE:

I have to see a sick friend at the county hospital.

*And she is gone.* Silva *has caught up to* Baby Doll *again.*

BABY DOLL:

You might as well shout at the moon as that old woman.

SILVA:

You didn't want her to go??

BABY DOLL:

She's got no business leaving me here alone.

SILVA:

It makes you uneasy to be alone here with me.

BABY DOLL:

I think she just pretended not to hear me. She has a passion for chocolate candy and she watches the news-papers like a hawk to see if anybody she knows is registered at the county hospital.

SILVA:

Hospital . . . ?

BABY DOLL:

They give candy to patients at the county hospital,

friends and relations send them flowers and candy and Aunt Rose Comfort calls on them and eats up their chocolate candy.

SILVA *explodes with laughter.*

BABY DOLL:

One time an old lady friend of Aunt Rose Comfort was dying at the county hospital and Aunt Rose Comfort went over and ate up a two-pound box of chocolate cherries while the old lady was dying, finished it all, hahahaha, while the old lady was dying.

*They're both laughing together.*

I like ole people—they're crazy. . . .

*They both laugh together. . . .*

SILVA:

Mrs. Meighan. . . . May I ask you something? Of a personal nature?

BABY DOLL:

What?

SILVA:

Are you really married to Mr. Meighan?

BABY DOLL:

Mr. Vacarro, that's a personal question.

SILVA:

All questions are more or less personal, Mrs. Meighan.

BABY DOLL:

Well, when I married I wasn't ready for marriage. I was still eighteen, but my daddy was practically on his death bed and wanted to see me took care of before he died. Well, ole Archie Lee had been hanging around like a sick dog for quite some time and . . . the boys are a sorry lot around here. Ask you to the movies and take you to the old rock quarry instead. You have to get out of the car and throw rocks at 'em, oh, I've had some experiences with boys that would curl your hair if I told you—some—experiences which I've had with boys!! But Archie Lee Meighan was an older fellow and in those days, well, his business was better. You hadn't put up that cotton gin of yours and Archie Lee was ginning out a lot of cotton. You remember?

SILVA:

Yes, I remember. . . .

BABY DOLL:

Well, I told my daddy I wasn't ready for marriage and my daddy told Archie Lee that I wasn't ready for it and he promised my daddy he'd wait till I was ready.

SILVA:

Then the marriage was postponed?

BABY DOLL:

Not the wedding, no, we had the wedding, my daddy gave me away. . . .

SILVA:

But you said that Archie Lee waited?

BABY DOLL:

Yes, *after* the wedding . . . he waited.

SILVA:

For what?

BABY DOLL:

For me to be ready for marriage.

SILVA:

How long did he have to wait?

BABY DOLL:

Oh, he's still waiting! Of course, we had an agreement that . . . well . . . I mean I told him that I'd be ready on my twentieth birthday—I mean ready or *not*. . . .

SILVA:

And that's tomorrow?

BABY DOLL:

Uh-huh.

SILVA:

And are you . . . will you—be ready?

BABY DOLL:

That all depends.

SILVA:

What on?

BABY DOLL:

Whether or not the furniture comes back—I guess. . . .

SILVA:

Your husband sweats more than any man I know and now I understand why!!

*There is a pause. They look at each other. Then* BABY DOLL *looks away. Then with a sudden access of energy she enters the house, slams the screen door in his face and latches it.*

BABY DOLL:

*There now! You wait out here! You just wait out here!*

SILVA:

*(Grinning at the screen door)*
Yes, ma'am. I will wait.

76]

## INTERIOR.  DIMLY LIT ENTRANCE HALL OF MEIGHAN HOUSE.

BABY DOLL *turns from screen door to porch and stumbles along the vast and shadowy hall towards the dim light of the kitchen. As soon as she disappears,* VACARRO *is seen through screen door. He jerks out a pocketknife and rips a hole in the screen.*

BABY DOLL *calls anxiously, out of sight.*

BABY DOLL:

(*From kitchen*)
*What's that?*

77]

## THE PORCH.

VACARRO *whistles loudly and casually on the porch. He now slips his fingers through the hole and lifts the latch.*

78]

## INTERIOR. KITCHEN OF MEIGHAN HOUSE. FULL SHOT.

*Large, old-fashioned room with antiquated, but very capacious, equipment—large ice-box, large sinks and draining boards, large stove converted to gas.*

BABY DOLL *stands in the middle of the floor with an apprehensive expression, but as* VACARRO *continues whistling on the porch, her usual placidity returns. She notices kettle of greens on the stove.*

BABY DOLL:

Stupid old thing—forgot to light the stove.

*She opens the ice-box for lemons.*

Git me a Frigidaire one of these days.

*The pan under the ice-box has overflowed and is swamping the floor.*

Got to empty that pan.

*Pulls it from under refrigerator with a grunt. A sound catches her ear, a sharp, slapping sound. She looks up anxiously, but the sound is not repeated. She takes out lemons, leaves ice-box door hanging open. All her movements are fumbling and weak. She keeps rubbing her perspiring hands on her hips. She starts to cut lemon, the knife slips and cuts her finger. She looks at the finger. It looks all right at first, then a drop of blood appears. She whimpers a little. The blood increases. She begins to cry like a baby.*

*She makes a vague, anxious movement. Again the slapping sound followed by a soft human sound like a chuckle. She looks that way. Cocks her head. But the sound is not repeated. Still squeezing the cut finger she begins to wander toward the front of the house.*

CAMERA PANS WITH BABY DOLL AS SHE WANDERS THROUGH HOUSE.

*She passes through a bare huge room with a dusty chandelier. It was the dining room when the house belonged to the old plantation owners. She whimpers under her breath, squeezing the bleeding finger. Now the blood is running down the hand to the wrist and down the wrist to the forearm and trickling into the soft hollow of her elbow. She groans and whimpers at the sight of the great flight of stairs, but starts up them.*

*Halfway up, at the landing, she hears the slapping*

*sound again and the faunlike mocking laughter. She
stops there and waits and listens—but the sound isn't
immediately repeated, so she goes on up.
She goes into the bathroom and starts to bandage her
cut finger.*

79]

INTERIOR HALL OF MEIGHAN HOUSE.
VACARRO DISCOVERED. FULL SHOT.
VACARRO *is grinning up at the staircase. He slaps the
banisters viciously with his whip, then chuckles.
CAMERA PANS WITH VACARRO.
He strolls into the kitchen, sees ice-box door hanging
open. Helps himself to the remains of a chicken, tear-
ing it apart and gnawing the meat off it. He notices
lemons and bloodspots—laughs.*

SILVA:

Trail o' blood! Ha ha!
*He empties the flooded ice-pan over dirty dishes in sink.*
Filth! Disgusting!
*He slaps the wall with whip and laughs.*

80]

INTERIOR. THE MEIGHANS' BEDROOM. BABY
DOLL WANDERS IN FROM BATHROOM.
*The finger is clumsily bandaged now, and she wanders
across the room and examines herself in the mirror.*

BABY DOLL:

Look 'a' me! Big mess. . . .
*There are dark stains of sweat on the watermelon pink
dress. She lazily starts to remove it. Hears the slapping*

Page 95

*sound and laugh closer. Pauses, her mouth hanging open. Fumbling attempt to lock door. Key slips from her weak, nerveless fingers. She stoops, grunting, to pick it up.*

81]

INTERIOR KITCHEN. VACARRO SQUEEZING LEMONS AND HURLING THE RINDS SAVAGELY AWAY.

*He finds gin bottle and sloshes gin into pitcher. Takes ice pick and chops off big hunk of ice. He seems to enjoy all these physical activities, grins tightly, exposing his teeth. Sticks ice pick into wall as if he were stabbing an enemy. Holds pitcher over his head whirling it rapidly so the drink sloshes over and ice rattles loudly, liquid running down his bare brown muscular arm. He drinks out of pitcher.*

82]

INTERIOR BEDROOM. BABY DOLL IN DAMP SLIP ROOTING IN CLOSET FOR A FRESH DRESS.

*She hears ice rattling in pitcher. Pauses. Cocks head, listening apprehensively. Makes sure door is locked.*

83]

INTERIOR MEIGHANS' BEDROOM—
A DIFFERENT ANGLE. BABY DOLL.

*Her slip hangs half off one great globular breast, gleaming with sweat. She listens intently.*

84]

INTERIOR HALL AND STAIRWAY OF MEIGHAN
HOUSE. VACARRO SOFTLY CLIMBING STAIRS.
*CAMERA FOLLOWS VACARRO INTO ROOMS
ACROSS HALL FROM BEDROOM—THEN INTO
CHILD'S NURSERY—*
> *Never used. Hobby horse, small fenced bed, Mother
> Goose pictures on wall. He sits astride wooden horse,
> lashes its rump with the whip and rocks on it.*

85]

INTERIOR MEIGHANS' BEDROOM. BABY DOLL
SPRINGS UP FROM FLOOR.
> Baby Doll *unlocks the door and peers anxiously into
> hall. The noise stops.*

BABY DOLL:
> Archie Lee! Is that you?
> Vacarro (*out of sight*) *gives a soft wolf-whistle.*

BABY DOLL:
> Who's that? Who's in there?
> *She crosses the hall into nursery.*

86]

INTERIOR NURSERY. VACARRO SLIPPING
INTO NEXT ROOM AS BABY DOLL ENTERS.

BABY DOLL:
> (*Nervously*)
> Hey! What's goin' on?
> Whip slap and soft mocking laughter, barely audible.

BABY DOLL:

Mr. Vacarro? Are you in that room?

*She crosses fearfully and enters next room,* VACARRO *slipping out just before her entrance. Now she is really frightened.*

87]

INTERIOR EMPTY ROOM ADJOINING NURSERY —FULL SHOT. BABY DOLL ENTERS FEARFULLY.

BABY DOLL:

You! Git outa my house! You got no right to come in! Where are you?

*The door to the hall is locked. She hears the key turn in the lock. Gasps. Pounds door. Rushes back panting into nursery.*

88]

INTERIOR NURSERY. BABY DOLL RUSHES IN.

BABY DOLL:

Mr. Vacarro, stop playing hide and seek!

*The soft mocking laughter comes from the hall.*

I know it's you! You're making me very nervous! Mr. Vacarro!! Mr. Vacarro. . . . Mr. Vacarro. . . .

*With each call she creeps forward a few steps. All of a sudden he springs at her, shouting—*

SILVA:

(*Sudden shout*)

BOO!

*At this point the scene turns into a wild romp of chil-*

Page 98

*dren. She shrieks with laughter. He howls, shouts. She shrieks with terror. She giggles hysterically, running into the hall and starting down steps.*

*He leaps upon banister and slides to foot of stairs. She turns on the stairs and runs through various rooms slamming doors, giggling hysterically as she runs. A spirit of abandon enters the flight and the pursuit. As he follows her into the bedroom, she throws a pillow at him. He does a comic pratfall, embracing the pillow. She shrieks with laughter. He lunges toward her, throwing the pillow at her fugitive figure.*

*She is about to run downstairs, but he blocks the way. She screams and takes the steps to the attic.*

89]

## INTERIOR ATTIC.

*Dusty late afternoon beams of light through tiny peaked windows in gables and a jumble of discarded things that have the poetry of things once lived with by the no-longer living.*

BABY DOLL *doesn't stop to observe all this. She probably didn't even expect to find herself in an attic. She rushes in, slams the door, discovers a rusty bolt and bolts it just as* VACARRO *arrives at the door.*

*Her panting laughter expires as he pushes the door. She suddenly realizes the full import of her situation; gasps and backs away.*

SILVA:

Open Sesame!!

BABY DOLL:

*(In a low, serious voice)*

The game is over. I've quit.

SILVA:

That's not fair, you've got to keep playing hide-and-seek till you're it.

BABY DOLL:

Mr. Vacarro, will you please go back downstairs so I can unlock the door of this attic and come out—because the floor is weak. . . . I don't want to fall through. It's crumbling under my feet. I had no idea—I never been up here before!—it was in such a weaken condition. *There is something appealing in her soft, pleasing voice.*

SILVA:

(*Whispering, mouth to crack*)

I wouldn't dream of leaving you alone in a falling-down attic any more than you'd dream of eatin' a nut a man had cracked in his mouth. Don't you realize that??

BABY DOLL:

(*With sudden gathering panic*)

Mr. Vacarro! I got to get out of here. Quick! Go! Go! —down! Quick, please!

SILVA:

I can hear that old floor giving away fast. . . .

BABY DOLL:

So can I, and I'm *on* it.

SILVA:

Shall I call the fire department to come here with a net to catch you when you fall through?

BABY DOLL:

Wouldn't be time. No! Go!—then I can unlock the——

SILVA:

No, I don't suppose they'd get here on time or if they

*Page 100*

did the net would be rotten as those fire hoses last night
when they came to put out the fire that burned down
my gin!

*Suddenly, a piece of plaster falls beneath her feet. The
rotten laths are exposed. She scrambles to another place,
which is—or seems—equally shaky. She screams.*

SILVA:

Are you being attacked by a ghost in there?

BABY DOLL:

Please be kind! Go away!

SILVA:

Why don't you unlock the door so I can come to your
rescue?

BABY DOLL:

I—can't because . . .

SILVA:

Huh? Huh?

BABY DOLL:

(*Whisper*)
YOU.

VACARRO *shoves door just a little with his shoulder. The
bolt is not strong.*

You . . . so! *Scare* me!

SILVA:

Scared of *me*??

BABY DOLL:

Yeah, scared of you and your—*whip.*

SILVA:

Why're you scared of my whip? Huh? Do you think I
might whip you? Huh? Scared I might whip you with
it and

*Slaps boots regularly with riding crop.*

leave red marks on your—body, on your—creamy white silk—skin? Is that why're scared, Mrs. Meighan?

*A murmur from her.*

You want me to go away—with my whip??

*Another murmur.*

All right. Tell you what I'm gonna do. I'm gonna slip pencil and paper under this door and all I want is your signature on the paper. . . .

BABY DOLL:

What paper?

SILVA:

I guess that you would call it an affidavit, legally stating that Archie Lee Meighan burned down the Syndicate Gin. . . .

(*Pause*)

Okay?

BABY DOLL:

Mr. Vacarro, this whole floor's about to collapse under me!

SILVA:

What do you say?

BABY DOLL:

Just leave the paper, leave it right out there and I'll sign it and send it to you, I'll . . .

SILVA:

Mrs. Meighan, I am a Sicilian. They're an old race of people, an ancient race, and ancient races aren't trustful races by nature. I've got to have the signed paper now. Otherwise I'm going to break this door down. Do you hear me?

*(A pause)*

Do you hear me?

*(Silence)*

*Whimpering, sobbing.*

I gather you don't believe me.

*Suddenly, with a single eloquent gesture of his whole body he has pushed the door open and on the other side* BABY DOLL, *in absolute panic, runs, runs away from the threatening man and whip and towards the darkest corner of the attic. A few steps, however, and the floor really gives way. There is a shower of plaster, a rising cloud of plaster dust.*

VACARRO's *face.*

*The dust settles to reveal her, precariously perched across a beam . . .*

VACARRO *calmly lights a cigarette.*

SILVA:

Now you're either going to agree to sign this thing, or I'm going to come out there after you and my additional weight will make the whole floor you know what!

BABY DOLL:

OOOOOOH! What am I gonna do?

SILVA:

Do what I tell you.

*(He gingerly steps on a place. . . . A trickle of plaster)*

Awful bad shape.

*He reaches and picks up a 1 x 3 about twelve feet long. On the end of it he puts a pencil and piece of paper.*

BABY DOLL:

O-o-o-o-o-h!

SILVA:

What?

*Suddenly, he stamps on the plaster. There is a big fall of plaster;* BABY DOLL *screams.*

BABY DOLL:

All right, all right. —All right. . . . Hurry! Hurry!

SILVA:

Hurry what?

BABY DOLL:

I'll do whatever you want—only hurry!!

SILVA:

Here it comes. . . .

*He reaches out his little piece of paper and pencil, balanced on the 1 x 3. She grabs it, scribbles her name in frantic haste, panting, and puts the piece of paper back, fixing it on a nail on the end of the 1 x 3, and* VACARRO *pulls it back. He looks at her signature and throws back his head in a sudden wild laugh.*

SILVA:

Thank you. You may come out now.

BABY DOLL:

Not till I hear you! Going down those stairs. . . .

SILVA:

(*Grinning and starting down*)

Hear me? Hear my descending footsteps on the stairs. . . .
VACARRO *straddles the long spiraled banister and slides all the way down to the landing at the bottom with a leap that starts another minor cascade.*

BABY DOLL *utters a little cry and comes out of the attic door. Silence. Putt-putt-putt-putt of the gin. She leans over stair well and looks straight down into the grin-*

*ning face of* VACARRO. *He gives her a quick, grinning nod or salute.*

SILVA:

Okay, you're "Home free"! And so am I! Bye-bye!

BABY DOLL:

Where are you going??

SILVA:

Back to my little gray Quonset home in the West! For a peaceful siesta. . . .

BABY DOLL:

Wait, please!—I want to——

*She starts to come running down the stairs, her hair wild, panting, sweating, smeared with attic dust. Then halfway down she stops. . . .*

BABY DOLL:

(*Now stealing towards him*)

I want to——

*But she can't remember what she "wants to." He waits quizzically with his cocky grin for her to complete her sentence but she doesn't. Instead she looks up and down him and her eyelids flutter as if the image could not be quietly contained.*

*He nods as if in agreement to something stated. He chuckles and then turns on his heels and starts briskly for the porch. She calls after him . . .*

BABY DOLL:

Was *that* all you wanted. . . ?

*He turns and looks at her.*

Me to confess that Archie Lee burnt down your gin?

SILVA:

What else did you imagine?

*She turns away like a shy child, serious-faced; she sits down on the bottom step.*

SILVA:

(*Gently*)

You're a child, Mrs. Meighan. That's why we played hide-and-seek, a game for children. . . .

BABY DOLL:

You don't have to go all the way to your place for a nap. You could take a nap here.

SILVA:

But all the furniture's been removed from the house.

BABY DOLL:

Not the nursery stuff. They's a small bed in there, a crib, you could curl up and—let the slats down. . . .

*An effect of two shy children trying to strike up a friendship. He continues to look at her. The windy afternoon has tossed a cloud over the sun, now declining. But it passes and his smile becomes as warm as sunlight. She isn't looking into his face but down at the scuffed kid slipper. Abruptly he gives a short quick nod and says simply . . .*

SILVA:

I'm happy to accept the invitation.

(*He starts up the stairs. When he gets to the point where she is sitting, he says*)

Come up and sing me to sleep.

(*Then he continues on up*)

BABY DOLL *is left alone, bewildered, sitting alone on the big staircase.*

BABY DOLL:

(*To herself*)

My daddy would *turn* in his *grave.*
*She starts up the stairs. . . .*

90]

THE NURSERY.

Vacarro *is on the crib, with the slats down. He is curled with his thumb in his mouth. She comes to view, stands in the doorway a moment, then goes and crouches beside the bed. Gently, she raises his head and bare throat, crooks an arm under and begins to sing: "Rock-a-Bye Baby."*

*He sighs contentedly, removes the signed paper from his shirt pocket and tucks it under his belt for safer keeping.*

*Then he appears to fall asleep.*

DISSOLVE.

91]

IN A HOSPITAL ROOM.

Aunt Rose Comfort *is sitting by a friend who is in her death coma.* Aunt Rose *eating chocolate cherries.*

DISSOLVE.

92]

SUPPLY STORE IN MEMPHIS.    MEIGHAN AT COUNTER.

ARCHIE:
    (*To clerk*)
    Godamighty man, I'm good for it.

*He reaches for the part he has come for. It's wrapped and ready to go.*

CLERK:

We have orders. No credit. Cash basis. Everything.

ARCHIE:

I warn you. I'll never come in this store again.

CLERK:

Sorry.

ARCHIE:

Look, I just happened to leave the place in my work clothes. My wallet ain't on me!

CLERK:

Cash only.

MR. ARCHIE LEE MEIGHAN *suddenly turns and leaves in complete disgust.*

93]

FRONT.  ARCHIE LEE'S GIN.

*It is several hours later and he has driven back from Memphis. He halts his motor with an exhausted grunt. He appears to have shrunk in size. He carries a sweat-drenched coat over his arm and the sweaty shirt clings to him. His chest heaves with unhealthy fast respiration, and he fingers the unbuttoned collar, as he takes in the situation: The gin is running again!!!—and without his o.k.—and how did they get the damned thing going again!!??*

93A]

INTERIOR GIN.

*He walks in and passes* ROCK.

*Page 108*

ARCHIE:

Hahaha! Looks like we're back in business.

ROCK:

(*Offers him only the most fleeting glance*)
Does, doesn't it.

ARCHIE:

You all must have done some mighty fast repairs.

ROCK:

No repairs—put in a new saw-cylinder.

ARCHIE:

From where? Out of a cloud? Why, I checked every supply outfit between Memphis and Greenville and nobody's got a new saw-cylinder ready for installation before next Wednesday.

ROCK:

(*Tersely*)
Boss had one at our place. I put it in.

ARCHIE:

How do you like that? How come I wasn't let in on this piece of information before I lit out of here on the wild-goose chase that just about killed me? Where is that wop Vacarro? I want to get some explanation of this.

*At this precise moment the whistle blows, announcing the end of the day and the gin machinery stops work. The Negroes, who have been working as porters and mechanics, line up for pay.*

ROCK:

(*Meantime*)
You seen the boss-man, Norm?

*A Negro shakes his head.*

ROCK *notices* ARCHIE *looking at the line a little worried.*

ROCK:

(*To Archie*)

Don't worry. Vacarro is meeting the payroll for tonight.

ARCHIE:

Where is he?

ROCK:

(*To another Negro*)

Moose, you seen the boss?

MOOSE:

No time lately, Capt'n.

94]

THE GIN.  (ANOTHER ANGLE)

MEIGHAN *retreats from the gin uncertainly. Camera follows.*

*Halfway across the road he hears laughter, evidently directed at him. His back stiffens. Something has happened, he feels, that has somehow made him the patsy of whatever occasion this is.*

95]

CLOSE SHOT.  MEIGHAN.

*Suspicious, angry, something violent and dangerous is growing up in his heart. He mutters to himself. Hears the laughter again. Curses to himself.*

96]

MEIGHAN ENTERS THE BIG FRONT YARD AND STARES AT THE HOUSE.

97]

THE HOUSE.
*Silent. Not a move. Not a sound.*

98]

MEIGHAN NOTICES VACARRO'S DISCARDED SHIRT.
*He picks it up and lifts his head and calls into the house.*

ARCHIE:
Hey! Anybody living here? Anybody still living in this house?

99]

UPSTAIRS. THE NURSERY.
BABY DOLL, *considerably disarrayed, has heard* ARCHIE'*s shout from below and is just making her way on hands and knees to the window. Now she crawls on the floor over to the crib.*

BABY DOLL:
It's Archie Lee.
*Downstairs screen door slams.* VACARRO *gurgles, murmurs, whimpers, all of which mean 'don't bother me, I want to sleep.'*
*There is a sudden shout from downstairs as if a cry of pain.*

100]

DOWNSTAIRS.
*What* MEIGHAN *sees is the debris of the ceiling. He looks up at the gaping hole in the roof over his head at*

*the top of the stair well and then down the stairs.* BABY
DOLL *appears on the staircase in a silken wrapper.*

ARCHIE:

*What happened here?*

BABY DOLL *doesn't answer. She stares at him with blank
insolence.*

ARCHIE:

Hunh? I said what the hell happened here?

BABY DOLL:

You mean that mess in the hall? The plaster broke in
the attic.

ARCHIE:

How'd that—how'd that—happen?

BABY DOLL:

How does anything happen? It just happened.
*She comes on lazily down, avoiding his look.*

101]

INTERIOR NIGHT. DOWNSTAIRS. FRONT
HALL.

ARCHIE:

Ain't I told you not to slop around here in a slip?
*She gives a faint indifferent shrug which enrages him;
he senses something openly contemptuous, a change in
her attitude towards him. He grabs her bare shoulder.*
What's the matter with your skin? It looks all broke
out.
*(Inspects the inflamed welts)*
What's this?

BABY DOLL:

What's what?

ARCHIE:

These marks on you?

BABY DOLL:

Mosquito bites, I scratched them. . . . Lemme go.

ARCHIE:

(*Bellowing*)

Ain't I told you not to slop around here in a slip???!!!
AUNT ROSE COMFORT, *alarmed by the shout, appears in
door to kitchen, crying out thin and high.*

AUNT ROSE:

Almost ready, now, folks, almost ready!!
*She rushes back into the kitchen with her frightened
cackle. There is a crash of china from the kitchen.*

ARCHIE:

The breakage alone in that kitchen would ruin a well-
to-do-man! Now you go up and git some decent clo'se
on yuh an' come back down. Y'know they got a new
bureau in Washington, D. C. It's called the U.W. Bureau. Y'know what U.W. stands for? It stands fo' useless women. They's secret plans on foot to round 'em all
up and shoot 'em. Hahahaha!

BABY DOLL:

How about men that's destructive? Don't they have secret plans to round up men that's destructive and shoot
them too?

ARCHIE:

What destructive men you talkin' about?

BABY DOLL:

Men that blow things up and burn things down because
they're too evil and stupid to git along otherwise. Because fair competition is too much for 'em. So they turn

criminal. Do things like Arson. Willful destruction of property by fire. . . .

*She steps out on the porch. Night sounds. A cool breeze tosses her damp curls. She sniffs the night air like a young horse. . . .*

*The porch light, a milky globe patterned with dead insects, turns on directly over her head and* ARCHIE LEE *comes up behind her and grips her bare shoulders, his face anxious, cunning.*

ARCHIE:

Who said that to you? Where'd you git that from??

BABY DOLL:

Turn that porch light off. There's men on the road can see me.

ARCHIE:

Who said *arson* to you? Who spoke of willful destruction of . . . YOU never knew them words. Who SAID 'em to yuh?

BABY DOLL:

Sometimes, Big Shot, you don't seem t' give me credit for much intelligence! I've been to school, in my life, and I'm a—magazine reader!

*She shakes off his grip and starts down porch steps. There is a group of men on Tiger Tail Road. One of them gives a wolf-whistle. At once,* ARCHIE LEE *charges down the steps and across the yard towards the road— crying out—*

ARCHIE:

*Who gave that whistle??* Which of you give a wolf-whistle at my wife?

*The group ignores him except for a light mocking laugh as they continue down road. The Camera returns to* BABY DOLL *blandly smiling.*

*We hear the rattle of the cistern pump being vigorously exercised in the side yard.* ARCHIE LEE *stalks back up to porch, winded, like an old hound....*

ARCHIE:

Men from the Syndicate *Plantation! White an' black* mixed! Headed fo' Tiger Tail Bayou with frog gigs and rubber boots on! I just hope they turn downstream and trespass across my property! I just hope they dast to! I'll blast them out of the Bayou with a shotgun!

BABY DOLL:

Small dogs have a loud bark.

ARCHIE:

Nobody's gonna insult no woman of *mine!!*

BABY DOLL:

You take a lot for granted when you say *mine.* This afternoon I come to you for protection. What did I *git? Slapped!* And told to go home.... I, for one, have got no sympathy for you, now or ever. An' the rasslin' match between us is *over* so let me *go!*

ARCHIE:

You're darn tootin' it's over. In just three hours the terms of the agreement will be settled for good.

BABY DOLL:

Don't count on it. That agreement is canceled. Because it takes two sides to make an agreement, like an argument, and both sides got to live up to it completely. You didn't live up to yours. Stuck me in a house which is haunted and five complete sets of unpaid-for furniture was removed from it las' night, OOHH I'm *free* from my side of that bargain!

ARCHIE:

*Sharp at midnight!* We'll find out about that.

BABY DOLL:

Too much has happened here lately. . . .

*She descends into yard.* ARCHIE LEE *eyes her figure, sweating, licking his chops.*

ARCHIE:

Well . . . my credit's wide open again!

BABY DOLL:

So is the jailhouse door wide open for you if the truth comes out.

ARCHIE:

You threatenin' me with—*blackmail??*

BABY DOLL:

Somebody's drawin' some cool well water from the pump back there.

*She starts back. He follows. The full frog-gigging moon emerges from a mackerel sky, and we see VA- CARRO making his ablutions at the cistern pump with the zest and vigor of a man satisfied.*

BABY DOLL:

(*With unaccustomed hilarity*)

HEIGH-HO SILVER . . . HaHa!!

ARCHIE LEE *stops dead in his tracks.*

ARCHIE:

Him?! Still on the place?

BABY DOLL:

Give me another drink of that sweet well water, will

yuh, Mistuh Vacarro? You're the first person could draw it.

ARCHIE:

(*Advancing*)

YOU STILL HERE?

BABY DOLL:

Archie Lee, Mr. Vacarro says he might not put up a new cotton gin, but let you gin cotton for him all the time, now. Ain't you pleased about that? Tomorrow he plans to come with lots more cotton, maybe another twenty-seven wagonloads. And while you're ginning it out, he'll have me entertain him, make lemonade for him. It's going to go on and on! Maybe even next fall.

SILVA:

(*Through the water*)

Good neighbor policy in practice.

(*Having wetted himself down he now drinks from gourd*)

I love well water. It tastes as fresh as if it never was tasted before. Mrs. Meighan, would you care for some, too?

BABY DOLL:

Why thank you, yes, I would.

*There is a grace and sweetness and softness of speech about her, unknown before. . . .*

SILVA:

Cooler nights have begun.

ARCHIE LEE *has been regarding the situation, with its various possibilities, and is far from content.*

ARCHIE:

How long you been on the place?

SILVA:

> (*Drawling sensuously with eyes on girl*)
> All this unusually long hot fall afternoon I've imposed
> on your hospitality. You want some of this well water?

ARCHIE:

> (*With a violent gesture of refusal*)
> Where you been here???

SILVA:

> Taking a nap on your only remaining bed. The crib in
> the nursery with the slats let down. I had to curl up on
> it like a pretzel, but the fire last night deprived me of
> so much sleep that almost any flat surface was suitable
> for slumber.
> (*Winks impertinently at* ARCHIE LEE, *then turns to grin
> sweetly at* BABY DOLL, *wiping the drippings of well
> water from his throat. Then turns back to* ARCHIE)
> But there's something sad about it. Know what I mean?

ARCHIE:

> Sad about what??

SILVA:

> An unoccupied nursery in a house, and all the other
> rooms empty....

ARCHIE:

> That's no problem of yours!

SILVA:

> The good neighbor policy makes your problems mine—
> and vice versa....

AUNT ROSE:

> (*Violent and high and shrill, from the back steps*)
> SUPPER! READY! CHILDREN....
> *She staggers back in.*

*Now there's a pause in which all three stand tense and silent about the water pump.* BABY DOLL *with her slow, new smile speaks up first. . . .*

BABY DOLL:

You all didn't hear us called in to supper?

ARCHIE:

You gonna eat here tonight?

SILVA:

Mrs. Meighan asked me to stay for supper but I told her I'd better get to hear the invitation from the head of the house before I'd feel free to accept it. So . . . What do you say?

*A tense pause . . . then, with great difficulty . . .*

ARCHIE:

Stay! . . . fo' supper.

BABY DOLL:

You'll have to take potluck.

SILVA:

I wouldn't be putting your out?

*This is addressed to* BABY DOLL, *who smiles vaguely and starts toward the house, saying . . .*

BABY DOLL:

I better get into mu' clo'se. . . .

ARCHIE:

Yeah . . . hunh. . . .

*They follow her sensuous departure with their eyes till she fades into the dusk.*

ARCHIE:

Did I understand you to say you wouldn't build a new gin but would leave your business to me?

*Page 119*

SILVA:

If that's agreeable with you. . . .

ARCHIE:

(*Turning from his wife's back to* VACARRO'S *face*)
I don't know yet, I'll have to consider the matter. . . .
Financing is involved such as—new equipment. . . .
Let's go in and eat now. I got a pain in my belly, I got
a sort of heartburn. . . .


102]

INTERIOR HOUSE.

*They enter the kitchen and then to the dining room.*
ARCHIE LEE'S *condition is almost shock. He can't quite
get with the situation. He numbly figures that he'd
better play it cool till the inner fog clears. But his in-
stinct is murder. His cowardly caution focuses his mal-
ice on the old woman and the unsatisfactory supper
she's prepared.*

ARCHIE:

Hey! Hey! One more place at the table! Mr. Vacarro
from the Syndicate Plantation is stayin' to supper.

AUNT ROSE:

(*With a startled outcry, clutching her chest*)
Oh—I had no idea that company was expected. Just let
me—change the silver and . . .

ARCHIE:

Another place is all that's called for. Have you been
here all day?

AUNT ROSE:

What was that, Archie Lee?

*Page 120*

ARCHIE:

HAVE YOU BEEN IN THE HOUSE ALL AFTER-
NOON OR DID YOU LIGHT OUT TO THE
COUNTY HOSPITAL TO EAT SOME CHOCO-
LATE CANDY????

AUNT ROSE *gasps as if struck, then she cackles* . . .

AUNT ROSE:

I—I—visited!—an old friend in a—coma!

ARCHIE:

Then you was out while I was——.

*(Turns to* VACARRO—*fiercely)*

I work like the hammers of hell! I come home to find
the attic floor has fell through, my wife bad-tempered,
insulting! and a supper of hog slops—. Sit down, eat.
I got to make a phone call.

*He crosses somewhat unsteadily into the hall and picks
up the telephone as* BABY DOLL *descends the grand
staircase and goes past him with face austerely averted.
She is clad in a fresh silk sheath and is adjusting an
earring as she passes through the hall. We go with her
into dining room.*

BABY DOLL:

He's at the phone about something and if I was you, I
wouldn't hang around long.

SILVA:

I think I've got the ace of spades in my pocket.

*He pats where he's stashed the confession signed by*
BABY DOLL.

BABY DOLL:

Don't count on a law court. Justice is deaf and blind
as that old woman!

AUNT ROSE COMFORT *rushes out to cut roses for a vase to set on table.*

BABY DOLL:

I'm advising you, go!—while he's on the phone.

SILVA:

I find you different this evening in some way.

BABY DOLL:

Never mind, just go! Before he gits off the phone.

SILVA:

Suddenly grown up!

BABY DOLL:

*(Looking at him gratefully)*

I feel cool and rested, for the first time in my life. I feel that way, rested and cool.

*(A pause)*

Are you going or staying???

*They are close together by table. Suddenly she catches her breath and flattens her body to his. The embrace is active. She reaches above her and pulls the beaded chain of the light bulb, plunging the room in dark. We hear two things: The breath of the embracing couple and the voice of* ARCHIE LEE *on the phone.*

ARCHIE:

A bunch of men from the Syndicate Plantation are out frog-giggin' on Tiger Tail Bayou and I thought we all might join the party. How's about meeting at the Brite Spot in halfn hour? With full equipment.

*A few more indistinct words, he hangs up. The light is switched back on in the dining room.* AUNT ROSE *rushes in.*

AUNT ROSE:

Roses! Poems of nature . . .

ARCHIE LEE *enters from the hall. His agitation is steadily mounting.*

ARCHIE:

Never mind poems of nature, just put food on th' table!

AUNT ROSE:

If I'd only known that company was expected, I'd . . .

*Her breathless voice expires as she scuttles about putting roses in a vase.*

AUNT ROSE:

Only take a minute.

ARCHIE:

We ain't waitin' no minute. Bring out the food. . . .

BABY DOLL *smiles, rather scornfully, at* ARCHIE LEE *bullying the old woman.*

ARCHIE:

Is that what they call a Mona Lisa smile you got on your puss?

BABY DOLL:

Don't pick on Aunt Rose. . . .

ARCHIE:

*(Shouting)*

Put some food on the table!!

*(Then muttering dangerously)*

I'm going to have a talk with that old woman, right here tonight. She's outstayed her welcome.

SILVA:

What a pretty blue wrapper you're wearing tonight, Mrs. Meighan.

BABY DOLL:
> *(Coyly)*
> Thank you, Mr. Vacarro.

SILVA:
> There's so many shades of blue. Which shade is that?

BABY DOLL:
> Just baby blue.

ARCHIE:
> Baby blue, huh!

SILVA:
> It brings out the blue of your eyes.

ARCHIE:
> *(Screaming)*
> Food! Food!

AUNT ROSE:
> Immediately! This instant!
> *She comes through door from the kitchen, holding a big plate of greens, which she sets on the table with great apprehension. They are not really cooked.* ARCHIE *stares at them.*

103]

CLOSE SHOT OF GREENS, WHICH ARE ALMOST RAW.

104]

CLOSE SHOT OF ARCHIE SWEARING UNDER HIS BREATH.

*Page 124*

## GROUP SCENE.

BABY DOLL:

This wrapper was part of my trousseau, as a matter of fact. I got all my trousseau at Memphis at various departments where my daddy was known. Big department stores on Main Street.

ARCHIE:

WHAT IS THIS STUFF??!! GRASS??!!

BABY DOLL:

Greens! Don't you know greens when you see them?

ARCHIE:

This stuff is greens??!!

AUNT ROSE *comes nervously from pantry.*

AUNT ROSE:

Archie Lee dotes on greens, don't you, Archie Lee?

ARCHIE:

No, I don't.

AUNT ROSE:

You don't? You don't dote on greens?

ARCHIE:

I don't think I ever declared any terrible fondness for greens in your presence.

AUNT ROSE:

Well, somebody did.

ARCHIE:

Somebody probably did—sometime, somewhere, but that don't mean it was me!

*Lurches back in his chair and half rises, swinging to*

*face* VACARRO—*who had taken* BABY DOLL'*s hand under the table.*

VACARRO *smiles blandly.*

BABY DOLL:

Sit back down, Big Shot, an' eat your greens. Greens puts iron in the system.

AUNT ROSE:

I thought that Archie Lee doted on greens! —All those likes an' dislikes are hard to keep straight in your head. But Archie Lee's easy to cook for. Jim's a complainer, oh, my, what a complainer Jim is, and Susie's household, they're nothing but complainers.

ARCHIE:

*Take this slop off th' table!!*

AUNT ROSE:

*(Terrified)*

I'll—cook you some—eggs Birmingham! —These greens didn' cook long enough. I played a fool trick with my stove. I forgot to light it! Ha ha! When I went out to the store—I had my greens on the stove. I thought I'd left 'em boilin'. But when I got home I discovered that my stove wasn't lighted.

ARCHIE:

Why do you say "my" stove? Why is everything "my"?

BABY DOLL:

Archie Lee, I believe you been drinkin'!

ARCHIE:

You keep out of this! Set down, Aunt Rose.

AUNT ROSE:

—Do what, Archie Lee?

*Page 126*

ARCHIE:

Set down here. I want to ask you a question.

AUNT ROSE *sits down slowly and stiffly, all atremble.*

What sort of—plans have you made?

AUNT ROSE:

Plans, Archie Lee? What sort of plans do you mean?

ARCHIE:

Plans for the future!

BABY DOLL:

I don't think this kind of discussion is necessary in front of company.

SILVA:

Mr. Meighan, when a man is feeling uncomfortable over something, it often happens that he takes out his annoyance on some completely innocent person just because he has to make somebody suffer.

ARCHIE:

You keep outa this, too. I'm askin' Aunt Rose a perfectly sensible question. Now, Aunt Rose. You been here since August and that's a mighty long stay. Now, it's my honest opinion that you're in need of a rest. You been cookin' around here and cookin' around there for how long now? How long have you been cookin' around people's houses?

AUNT ROSE:

*(Barely able to speak)*

I've helped out my—relatives, my—folks—whenever they —*needed me to!* I was always—*invited!* Sometimes—*begged* to come! When *babies* were expected or when somebody was *sick,* they called for Aunt Rose, and

Aunt Rose was always—ready. . . . Nobody *ever* had to
—*put me—out!* —If you—gentlemen will excuse me
from the table—I will pack my things! If I hurry I'll
catch the nine o'clock bus to——

*She can't think 'where to.'* VACARRO *seizes her hand,
pushing back from table.*

SILVA:

Miss Rose Comfort. Wait. I'll drive you home.

AUNT ROSE:

—I don't!—have nowhere to!—go. . . .

SILVA:

Yes, you do. I need someone to cook for me at my
place. I'm tired of my own cooking and I am anxious
to try those eggs Birmingham you mentioned. Is it a
deal?

AUNT ROSE:

—Why, I——

BABY DOLL:

Sure it's a deal. Mr. Vacarro will be good to you, Aunt
Rose Comfort, and he will even *pay* you, and maybe—
well—y'never can tell about things in the future. . . .

AUNT ROSE:

*I'll run pack my things!*
*She resumes reedy hymn in a breathless, cracked voice
as she goes upstairs.*

ARCHIE:

Anything else around here you wanta take with yuh,
Vacarro?

SILVA:

*(Looks around coolly as if considering the question)*

*Page 128*

BABY DOLL:

   *(Utters a high, childish giggle)*

ARCHIE:

   Well, *is* they? Anything else around here you wanta take away with yuh?

BABY DOLL:

   *(Rising gaily)*

   Why, yaiss, Archie Lee. Mr. Vacarro noticed the house was overloaded with furniture and he would like us to loan him five complete sets of it to——

ARCHIE:

   *(Seizing neck of whiskey bottle)*

   YOU SHUDDUP! I will git to you later.

BABY DOLL:

   If you ever git to me it sure is going to be *later,* ha ha, *much* later, ha ha!

   *She crosses to kitchen sink, arranging her kiss-me-quicks in the soap-splashed mirror, also regarding the two men behind her with bland satisfaction: her childish face, beaming, is distorted by the flawed glass.*

   *She sings or hums "Sweet and Lovely." ARCHIE LEE stands by table, breathing heavy as a walrus in labor. He looks from one to the other. SILVA coolly picks up a big kitchen knife and lops off a hunk of bread, then tosses kitchen knife out of ARCHIE LEE's reach and then he dips bread in pot of greens.*

SILVA:

   Colored folks call this pot liquor.

BABY DOLL:

   I love pot liquor.

SILVA:

Me, too.

BABY DOLL:

(*Dreamily*)

—Crazy 'bout pot liquor. . . .

*She turns about and rests her hips against sink.* ARCHIE
LEE's *breathing is loud as a cotton gin, his face fiery.
He takes swallow after swallow from bottle.*

VACARRO *devours bread.*

SILVA:

Mm-*UMMM!*

BABY DOLL:

Good?

SILVA:

*Yes!—Good!*

BABY DOLL:

—*That's* good. . . .

OLD FUSSY *makes a slow stately entrance, pushing the
door open wider with her fat hips and squawking peev-
ishly at this slight inconvenience.*


MEIGHAN *wheels about violently and hurls empty bottle
at her. She flaps and squawks back out. Her distressed
outcries are taken up by her sisters, who are sensibly
roosting.*

BABY DOLL:

(*Giggling*)

Law! Ole Fussy mighty near made it that time! Why,
that old hen was comin' in like she'd been invited t'supper.

*Page 130*

*Her giggly voice expires as* MEIGHAN *wheels back around and bellows.*

ARCHIE LEE *explodes volcanically. His violence should give him almost a Dostoevskian stature.*

*It builds steadily through scene as a virtual lunacy possesses him with realization of his hopeless position.*

ARCHIE:

*OH HO HO HO HO!*

*(Kicks kitchen door shut)*

Now you all listen to me! Quit giving looks back an' forth an' listen to me! Y'think I'm deaf, dumb an' blind or somethin', do yuh? You're *mistook,* Oh, brother, but you're much, much—*mistook!* Ohhhh, I knooow!—I guess I look like a—I guess I look like a——
*Panting, puffing pause; he reels a little, clutching chair back.*

BABY DOLL:

*(Insolently childish lisp)*

What d'you guess you look like, Archie Lee? Y'was about t' tell us an' then yuh quit fo' some——

ARCHIE:

*Yeah, yeah, yeah!* Some little innocent Baby Doll of a wife not ready fo' marriage, oh, no, not yet ready for marriage but plenty ready t'—— Oh, I see how it's funny, I can see how it's funny, I see the funny side of it. *Oh ho ho ho ho!* Yes, it sure is comic, comic as hell! But there's one little *teensy-eensy* little—thing that you —*overlooked!* I! Got *position!* Yeah, yeah, *I* got *position!* Here in this county! Where I was bo'n an' brought up! I hold a respected position, lifelong!—member of—— Wait! Wait!—Baby Doll. . . .

*She had started to cross past him; he seizes her wrist.*
*She wrenches free.* VACARRO *stirs and tenses slightly but*
*doesn't rise or change his cool smile.*

On my side 're friends, long-standin' *bus'ness* associates,
an' *social!* See what I mean? You ain't got that advan-
tage, have you, mister? Huh, mister? Ain't you a dago,
or something, excuse me, I mean Eyetalian or something, here in Tiger Tail County?

SILVA:

Meighan, I'm not a doctor, but I was a medical corps-
man in the Navy and you've got a very unhealthy looking flush on your face right now which is almost purple
as a——

*He was going to say 'baboon's behind.'*

ARCHIE:

*(Bellowing out)*
ALL I GOT TO DO IS GIT ON THAT PHONE
IN THE HALL!

SILVA:

And call an ambulance from the county hospital?

ARCHIE:

Hell, I don't even need t' make a phone call! I can
handle this situation *m'self!*—with legal protection that
no one could——

SILVA:

*(Still coolly)*
What situation do you mean, Meighan?

ARCHIE:

Situation which I come home to find here under my
roof! Oh, I'm not such a marble-missing old fool!—I

couldn't size it up!—I sized it up the moment I seen you was still on this place and *her!*—with that *sly smile on her!*

*(Takes a great swallow of liquor from the fresh bottle)*

And *you* with *yours* on *you!* I know how to wipe off both of those sly——!

*Crosses to closet door.* BABY DOLL *utters a gasp and signals* VACARRO *to watch out.*

VACARRO *rises calmly.*

SILVA:

Meighan?

*(He speaks coolly, almost with a note of sympathy)*

*Y*ou know, and *I* know, and I *know* that you *know* that I *know!*—That you set fire to my cotton gin last night. You burnt down the Syndicate Gin and I got in my pocket a signed affidavit, a paper, signed by a witness, whose testimony will even hold up in the law courts of Tiger Tail County!—That's all I come here for and that's all I got . . . whatever else you suspect— well!—you're mistaken. . . . Isn't that so, Mrs. Meighan? Isn't your husband mistaken in thinking that I got anything out of this place but this signed affidavit which was the purpose of my all-afternoon call?

*She looks at him, angry, hurt.*

MEIGHAN *wheels about, panting.*

SILVA:

*(Continuing)*

Yes, I'm foreign but I'm not revengeful, Meighan, at least not more than is rightful.

*(Smiles sweetly)*

—I think we got a workable good neighbor policy between us. It might work out, anyhow I think it deserves a try. Now as to the other side of the situation, which I don't have to mention. Well, all I can say is, a certain attraction—exists! Mutually, I believe! But nothing's been rushed. I needed a little shut-eye after last night's —excitement. I took a nap upstairs in the nursery crib with the slats let down to accommodate my fairly small frame, and I have faint recollection of being sung to by someone—a lullaby song that was—sweet . . .

*(His voice is low, caressing)*

—and the touch of—cool fingers, but that's all, absolutely!

ARCHIE:

Y'think I'm gonna put up with this——?

SILVA:

Situation? You went to a whole lot of risk an' trouble to get my business back. Now don't you want it? It's up to you, Archie Lee, it's——

ARCHIE:

COOL! Yeah, cool, very cool!

SILVA:

—The heat of the fire's died down. . . .

ARCHIE:

UH—HUH! YOU'VE FIXED YOUR WAGON! WITH THIS SMART TALK, YOU JUST NOW FIXED YOUR WAGON! I'M GONNA MAKE A PHONE CALL THAT'LL WIPE THE GRIN OFF YOUR GREASY WOP FACE FOR GOOD!

*He charges into hall and seizes phone.*

SILVA:

*(Crossing to* BABY DOLL *at kitchen sink)*

Is my wop face greasy, Mrs. Meighan?

*She remains at mirror but her childish smile fades: her face goes vacant and blind: she suddenly tilts her head back against the bare throat of the man standing behind her. Her eyes clenched shut. . . .*

*His eyelids flutter as his body presses against all the mindless virgin softness of her abundant young flesh. We can't see their hands, but hers are stretched behind her, his before him.*

106]

HALL.

ARCHIE:

*(Bellowing like a steer)*
I WANT SPOT, MIZZ HOPKINS, WHE' IS SPOT!?

107]

BABY DOLL WITH VACARRO.

BABY DOLL:

I think you better go 'way. . . .

SILVA:

I'm just waiting to take you girls away with me. . . .

BABY DOLL:

*(Softly as in a dream)*
Yeah. I'm goin' too. I'll check in at the Kotton King Hotel and—— Now I better go up an'—he'p Aunt Rose Comfo't pack. . . .

*Releases herself regretfully from the embrace and crosses into hall.*

HALL. CLOSE SHOT OF SILVA LOOKING AFTER HER. IN THE HALL SHE UTTERS A SHARP OUTCRY AS MEIGHAN STRIKES AT HER.

BABY DOLL:

YOU GONNA BE SORRY FOR EV'RY TIME YOU LAID YOUR UGLY OLE HANDS ON ME, YOU STINKER, YOU! YOU STINKING STINKER, STINKERRR!

*Her footsteps running upstairs.* VACARRO *chuckles almost silently and goes quietly out the back door.*

109]

THE YARD.

VACARRO *crosses through a yard littered with uncollected garbage, tin cans, refuse. . . .*

110]

HALL. MEIGHAN REMOVES SHOTGUN FROM CLOSET.

111]

YARD. CUT BACK TO EXTERIOR.

*Crooked moon beams fitfully through a racing mackerel sky, the airs full of motion.*

VACARRO *picks his way fastidiously among the refuse, wades through the tall seeding grass, into the front yard. Clutches the lower branch of a pecan tree and swings up into it. Cracks a nut between his teeth as—*

ARCHIE:

*(Shouting and blundering through the house)*
HEY! WHERE YOU HIDING? WHERE YOU
HIDING, WOP?!

112]

HOUSE. CLOSE SHOT OF MEIGHAN WITH
SHOTGUN AND LIQUOR BOTTLE, ALREADY
STUMBLING DRUNK. . . .

113]

YARD. EXTERIOR NIGHT. VACARRO IN TREE.
VOICE OF BABY DOLL AT PHONE.

BABY DOLL:

I want the Police Chief. Yes, the Chief, not just the
police, the Chief. This is Baby Doll McCorkle speaking, the ex-Mrs. Meighan on Tiger Tail Road! My husband has got a shotgun and is threat'nin' to——
*Her voice turns into a scream. She comes running out
front door followed by* MEIGHAN. *She darts around side
of house.* MEIGHAN *is very drunk now. He goes the
opposite way around the house.* VACARRO *drops out of
tree and gives* BABY DOLL *a low whistle. She rushes
back to front yard.*

BABY DOLL:

*Oh, Gah, Gah, watch out, he's got a shotgun. He's—
crazy! I callt th' Chief of——*
VACARRO *leaps into tree again.*

SILVA:

Grab my hand! Quick! Now *up! Up,* now Baby Doll!

*He hoists her into tree with him as the wild-eyed old bull comes charging back around house with his weapon. He blasts away at a shadow. (Yard is full of windy shadows.) He is sobbing.*

ARCHIE:

BABY DOLL! BABY! BABY! BABY DOLL! MY BABY!

*Goes stumbling around back of house, great wind in the trees.* BABY DOLL *rests in the arms of* VACARRO.

MEIGHAN *in back yard. Storm cellar door bangs open. Meighan fires through it. Then at chicken coop. Then into wheelless limousine chassis in side yard, etc., etc.*

*Shot of* VACARRO *and* BABY DOLL *in fork of pecan tree.*

SILVA:

*(Grinning)*

We're still playing hide-and-seek!

BABY DOLL:

*(Excitedly, almost giggling)*

How long you guess we gonna be up this tree?

SILVA:

I don't care. I'm *comfortable*—Are you?

*Her answer is a sigh. He cracks a nut in his mouth and divides it with her. She giggles and whispers: "Shhhh!"*

ARCHIE:

*(Raving, sobbing, stumbling)*

Baby, my baby, oh, Baby Doll, my baby. . . .

*Silence.*

HEY! WOP! YELLOWBELLY! WHERE ARE YUH?

*Page 138*

AUNT ROSE COMFORT *comes forlornly out on the porch, weighed down by ancient suitcase, roped together.*

AUNT ROSE:

*(Fearfully, her hair blown wild by the wind)*
Baby Doll, honey? Honey? Baby Doll, honey?

ARCHIE:

*(In back yard)*
I SEE YOU! COME OUT OF THERE, YOU YEL-LOWBELLY WOP, YOU!

*Shotgun blasts away behind house.* AUNT ROSE COMFORT *on front porch utters a low cry and drops her suitcase. Backs against wall, hand to chest.*

*Fade in police siren approaching down Tiger Tail Road.*

BABY DOLL:

*(Nestling in* VACARRO's *arms in tree)*
I feel sorry for poor old AUNT ROSE COMFORT. She doesn't know where to go or what to do. . . .

*Moon comes briefly out and shines on their crouched figures in fork on tree.*

SILVA:

*(Gently)*
Does anyone know where to go, or what to do?

114]

THE YARD. ANOTHER ANGLE. POLICE CAR STOPPING BEFORE THE HOUSE AND MEN JUMPING OUT.

*Shot of* MEIGHAN *staggering and sobbing among the litter of uncollected garbage.*

ARCHIE:

Baby Doll, my baby! Yellow son of a——

115]

THE YARD. ANOTHER ANGLE. SHOT OF AUNT
ROSE COMFORT RETREATING INTO SHADOW
AS POLICE COME AROUND THE HOUSE
SUPPORTING ARCHIE LEE'S LIMP FIGURE.
SHOT OF COUPLE IN TREE AS MOON GOES
BACK OF CLOUDS.

*Stillness. Dark.* AUNT ROSE COMFORT *begins to sing a
hymn: "Rock of Ages."*

AUNT ROSE:

Rock of ages, cleft for me,
Let me hide myself in Thee!

VACARRO *drops out of tree and stands with arms lifted
for* BABY DOLL.

# 27 *Wagons Full of Cotton*

## A Mississippi Delta Comedy

*"Now Eros shakes my soul, a wind on the mountain, falling on the oaks."*

SAPPHO

## THE CHARACTERS

JAKE MEIGHAN, *a cotton-gin owner.*

FLORA MEIGHAN, *his wife.*

SILVA VICARRO, *superintendent of the Syndicate Plantation.*

*All of the action takes place on the front porch of the Meighans' residence near Blue Mountain, Mississippi.*

SCENE:

*The front porch of the Meighans' cottage near Blue Mountain, Mississippi. The porch is narrow and rises into a single narrow gable. There are spindling white pillars on either side supporting the porch roof and a door of Gothic design and two Gothic windows on either side of it. The peaked door has an oval of richly stained glass, azure, crimson, emerald, and gold. At the windows are fluffy white curtains gathered coquettishly in the middle by baby-blue satin bows. The effect is not unlike a doll's house.*

## Scene I

*It is early evening and there is a faint rosy dusk in the sky. Shortly after the curtain rises,* Jake Meighan, *a fat man of sixty, scrambles out the front door and races around the corner of the house carrying a gallon can of coal oil. A dog barks at him. A car is heard starting and receding rapidly in the distance. A moment later* Flora *calls from inside the house.*

FLORA:

Jake! I've lost m' white kid purse!

*Closer to the door.*

Jake? Look'n see 'f uh laid it on th' swing.

*There is a pause.*

Guess I could've left it in th' Chevy?

*She comes up to screen door.*

Jake. Look'n see if uh left it in th' Chevy. Jake?

*She steps outside in the fading rosy dusk. She switches on the porch light and stares about, slapping at gnats attracted by the light. Locusts provide the only answering voice.* Flora *gives a long nasal call.*

Ja-ay—a-a-ake!

*A cow moos in the distance with the same inflection. There is a muffled explosion somewhere about half a mile away. A strange flickering glow appears, the reflection of a burst of flame. Distant voices are heard exclaiming.*

VOICES:

*(Shrill, cackling like hens)*

You heah that noise?

Yeah! Sound like a bomb went off!

Oh, look!

Why, it's a fire!

Where's it at? You tell?

Th' Syndicate Plantation!

Oh, my God! Let's go!

*A fire whistle sounds in the distance.*

Henry! Start th' car! You all wanta go with us?

Yeah, we'll be right out!

Hurry, honey!

*A car can be heard starting up.*

Be right there!

Well, hurry.

VOICE:

(*Just across the dirt road*)

Missus Meighan?

FLORA:

Ye-ah?

VOICE:

Ahn't you goin' th' fire?

FLORA:

I wish I could but Jake's gone off in th' Chevy.

VOICE:

Come awn an' go with us, honey!

FLORA:

Oh, I cain't an' leave th' house wide open! Jake's gone off with th' keys. What do you all think it is on fire?

VOICE:

Th' Syndicate Plantation!

FLORA:

Th' Syndicate Plan-*ta*-tion?

*The car starts off and recedes.*

Oh, my Go-od!

*She climbs laboriously back up on the porch and sits on the swing which faces the front. She speaks tragically to herself.*

Nobody! Nobody! Never! Never! Nobody!

*Locusts can be heard. A car is heard approaching and stopping at a distance back of house. After a moment* JAKE *ambles casually up around the side of the house.*

FLORA:

(*In a petulant babyish tone*)
*Well!*

JAKE:

Whatsamatter, baby?

FLORA:

I never known a human being could be that mean an' thoughtless!

JAKE:

Aw, now, that's a mighty broad statement fo' you to make, Mrs. Meighan. What's the complaint this time?

FLORA:

Just flew out of the house without even sayin' a word!

JAKE:

What's so bad about that?

FLORA:

I told you I had a headache comin' on an' had to have a dope, there wassen a single bottle lef' in th' house, an' you said, Yeah, get into yuh things 'n' we'll drive in town right away! So I get into m' things an' I cain't find m' white kid purse. Then I remember I left it on th' front seat of th' Chevy. I come out here t' git it. Where are you? Gone off! Without a word! Then there's a big explosion! Feel my heart!

JAKE:

Feel my baby's heart?

*He puts a hand on her huge bosom.*

FLORA:

Yeah, just you feel it, poundin' like a hammer! How'd I know what happened? You not here, just disappeared somewhere!

JAKE:

(*Sharply*)

Shut up!

*He pushes her head roughly.*

FLORA:

Jake! What did you do that fo'?

JAKE:

I don't like how you holler! Holler ev'ry thing you say!

FLORA:

What's the matter with you?

JAKE:

Nothing's the matter with me.

FLORA:

Well, why did you go off?

JAKE:

I didn' go off!

FLORA:

You certainly *did* go off! Try an' tell me that you never went off when I just now seen an' heard you drivin' back in th' car? What uh you take me faw? No sense a-tall?

JAKE:

If you got sense you keep your big mouth shut!

FLORA:

Don't talk to me like that!

JAKE:

Come on inside.

FLORA:

I won't. Selfish an' inconsiderate, that's what you are! I told you at supper, There's not a bottle of Coca-Cola left on th' place. You said, Okay, right after supper we'll drive on over to th' White Star Drugstore an' lay in a good supply. When I come out of th' house—

JAKE:

(*He stands in front of her and grips her neck with both hands.*)

Look here! Listen to what I tell you!

FLORA:

*Jake!*

JAKE:

Shhh! Just listen, baby.

FLORA:

Lemme go! G'damn you, le' go my throat!

JAKE:

Jus' try an' concentrate on what I tell yuh!

FLORA:

Tell me what?

JAKE:

I ain't been off th' po'ch.

FLORA:

Huh!

JAKE:

I ain't been off th' front po'ch! Not since supper! Understand that, now?

FLORA:

Jake, honey, you've gone out of you' mind!

JAKE:

Maybe so. Never you mind. Just get that straight an' keep it in your haid. I ain't been off the porch of this house since supper.

FLORA:

But you sure as God *was* off it!

*He twists her wrist.*

Ouuuu! Stop it, stop it, stop it!

JAKE:

Where have I been since supper?

FLORA:

Here, here! on th' porch! Fo' God's sake, quit that twistin'!

JAKE:

Where have I been?

FLORA:

Porch! Porch! Here!

JAKE:

Doin' what?

FLORA:

*Jake!*

JAKE:

Doin' what?

FLORA:

Lemme go! Christ, Jake! Let loose! Quit twisting, you'll break my wrist!

JAKE:

(*Laughing between his teeth*)

Doin' what? What doin'? Since supper?

FLORA:

*(Crying out)*
How in hell do I know!

JAKE:

'Cause you was right here with me, all the time, for every second! You an' me, sweetheart, was sittin' here together on th' swing, just swingin' back an' forth every minute since supper! You got that in your haid good now?

FLORA:

*(Whimpering)*
Le'-go!

JAKE:

Got it? In your haid good now?

FLORA:

Yeh, yeh, yeh—leggo!

JAKE:

What was I doin', then?

FLORA:

Swinging! For Christ's sake—swingin'!
*He releases her. She whimpers and rubs her wrist but the impression is that the experience was not without pleasure for both parties. She groans and whimpers. He grips her loose curls in his hand and bends her head back. He plants a long wet kiss on her mouth.*

FLORA:

*(Whimpering)*
Mmmm-hmmmm! Mmmm! Mmmm!

JAKE:

*(Huskily)*
Tha's my swee' baby girl.

FLORA:

Mmmmm! Hurt! Hurt!

JAKE:

Hurt?

FLORA:

Mmmm! Hurt!

JAKE:

Kiss?

FLORA:

Mmmm!

JAKE:

Good?

FLORA:

Mmmm . . .

JAKE:

Good! Make little room.

FLORA:

Too hot!

JAKE:

Go on, make little room.

FLORA:

Mmmmm . . .

JAKE:

Crosspatch?

FLORA:

Mmmmmm.

JAKE:

Whose baby? Big? Sweet?

FLORA:

Mmmmm! Hurt!

JAKE:

Kiss!

*He lifts her wrist to his lips and makes gobbling sounds.*

FLORA:

(*Giggling*)

Stop! Silly! Mmmm!

JAKE:

What would I do if you was a big piece of cake?

FLORA:

Silly.

JAKE:

Gobble! Gobble!

FLORA:

Oh, you—

JAKE:

What would I do if you was angel food cake? Big white piece with lots of nice thick icin'?

FLORA:

(*Giggling*)

Quit!

JAKE:

Gobble, gobble, gobble!

FLORA:

(*Squealing*)

Jake!

JAKE:

Huh?

FLORA:

You *tick*-le!

JAKE:

Answer little question!

FLORA:

Wh-at?

JAKE:

Where I been since supper?

FLORA:

Off in the Chevy!

*He instantly seizes the wrist again. She shrieks.*

JAKE:

Where've I been since supper?

FLORA:

Po'ch! Swing!

JAKE:

Doin' what?

FLORA:

*Swingin'!* Oh, Christ, Jake, let loose!

JAKE:

Hurt?

FLORA:

Mmmmm . . .

JAKE:

Good?

FLORA:

(*Whimpering*)

Mmmmm . . .

JAKE:

Now you know where I been an' what I been doin' since supper?

FLORA:

Yeah . . .

JAKE:

Case anybody should ask?

FLORA:

Who's going to ast?

JAKE:

Never mind who's goin' t' ast, just you know the answers! Uh-huh?

FLORA:

Uh-huh.

*Lisping babyishly.*

This is where you been. Settin' on th' swing since we had supper. Swingin'—back an' fo'th—back an' fo'th. . . . You didn' go off in th' Chevy.

*Slowly.*

An' you was awf'ly surprised w'en th' Syndicate fire broke out!

JAKE *slaps her.*

Jake!

JAKE:

Everything you said is awright. But don't you get ideas.

FLORA:

Ideas?

JAKE:

A woman like you's not made to have ideas. Made to be hugged an' squeezed!

FLORA:

(*Babyishly*)

Mmmm . . .

JAKE:

But not for ideas. So don't you have ideas.

*He rises.*

Go out an' get in th' Chevy.

Page 154

FLORA:

We goin to th' fire?

JAKE:

No. We ain' goin' no fire. We goin' in town an' get us a case a dopes because we're hot an' thirsty.

FLORA:

(*Vaguely, as she rises*)

I lost m' white—kid—purse . . .

JAKE:

It's on the seat of th' Chevy whe' you left it.

FLORA:

Whe' *you* goin'?

JAKE:

I'm goin in t' th' toilet. I'll be right out.

*He goes inside, letting the screen door slam.* FLORA *shuffles to the edge of the steps and stands there with a slight idiotic smile. She begins to descend, letting herself down each time with the same foot, like a child just learning to walk. She stops at the bottom of the steps and stares at the sky, vacantly and raptly, her fingers closing gently around the bruised wrist.* JAKE *can be heard singing inside.*

> "My baby don' care fo' rings
> Or other expensive things—
> My baby just cares—fo'—me!"

## SCENE II

*It is just after noon. The sky is the color of the satin bows on the window curtains—a translucent, innocent blue. Heat devils are shimmering over the flat Delta country and the peaked white front of the house is like a shrill exclamation. Jake's gin is busy; heard like a steady pulse across the road. A delicate lint of cotton is drifting about in the atmosphere.*

*J*AKE *appears, a large and purposeful man with arms like hams, covered with a fuzz of fine blond hair. He is followed by* S*ILVA* V*ICARRO* *who is the superintendent of the Syndicate Plantation where the fire occurred last night.* V*ICARRO* *is a rather small and wiry man of dark Latin looks and nature. He wears whipcord breeches, laced boots, and a white undershirt. He has a Roman Catholic medallion on a chain about his neck.*

JAKE:

(*With the good-natured condescension of a very large man for a small one*)

Well, suh, all I got to say is you're a mighty lucky little fellow.

VICARRO:

Lucky? In what way?

JAKE:

That I can take on a job like this right now! Twenty-seven wagons full of cotton's a pretty big piece of bus'ness, Mr. Vicarro.

*Stopping at the steps.*

*Baby!*

*He bites off a piece of tobacco plug.*

What's yuh firs' name?

VICARRO:

Silva.

JAKE:

How do you spell it?

VICARRO:

S-I-L-V-A.

JAKE:

Silva! Like a silver lining! Ev'ry cloud has got a silver lining. What does that come from? The Bible?

VICARRO:

(*Sitting on the steps*)

No. The Mother Goose Book.

JAKE:

Well, suh, you sure are lucky that I can do it. If I'd been busy like I was two weeks ago I would've turned it down. *BABY! COME OUT HERE A MINUTE!* *There is a vague response from inside.*

VICARRO:

Lucky. Very lucky.

*He lights a cigarette.* FLORA *pushes open the screen door and comes out. She has on her watermelon-pink silk dress and is clutching against her body the big white kid purse with her initials on it in big nickel plate.*

JAKE:

(*Proudly*)

Mr. Vicarro—I want you to meet Mrs. Meighan. Baby, this is a very down-at-the-mouth young fellow I want you to cheer up fo' me. He thinks he's out of luck because his cotton gin burnt down. He's got twenty-seven wagons full of cotton to be ginned out on a hurry-up order from his most impo'tant customers in Mobile. Well, suh, I said to him, Mr. Vicarro, you're to be congratulated—not because it burnt down, but because I happen to be in a situation to take the business over. Now you tell him just how lucky he is!

FLORA:

(*Nervously*)

Well, I guess he don't see how it was lucky to have his gin burned down.

VICARRO:

(*Acidly*)

No, ma'am.

JAKE:

(*Quickly*)

Mr. Vicarro. Some fellows marry a girl when she's little an' tiny. They like a small figure. See? Then, when the girl gets comfo'tably settled down—what does she do? Puts on flesh—of cou'se!

FLORA:

(*Bashfully*)

Jake!

JAKE:

Now then! How do they react? Accept it as a matter of cou'se, as something which 'as been ordained by nature? Nope! No, suh, not a bit! They sta't to feeling abused. They think that fate must have a grudge against them because the little woman is not so little as she used to be. Because she's gone an' put on a matronly figure. Well, suh, that's at the root of a lot of domestic trouble. However, Mr. Vicarro, I never made that mistake. When I fell in love with this baby doll I've got here, she was just the same size then that you see her today.

FLORA:

(*Crossing shyly to porch rail*)

Jake . . .

JAKE:

(*Grinning*)

A woman not large but tremendous! That's how I liked her—tremendous! I told her right off, when I slipped th' ring on her finger, one Satiddy night in a boathouse on Moon Lake—I said to her, honey, if you take off one single pound of that body—I'm going to quit yuh! I'm going to quit yuh, I said, the minute I notice you've started to take off weight!

FLORA:

Aw, Jake—please!

JAKE:

I don't want nothing little, not in a woman. I'm not after nothing *petite,* as the Frenchmen call it. This is what I wanted—and what I *got!* Look at her, Mr. Vicarro. Look at her blush!

*He grips the back of* FLORA's *neck and tries to turn her around.*

FLORA:

Aw, quit, Jake! Quit, will yuh?

JAKE:

See what a doll she is?

FLORA *turns suddenly and spanks him with the kid purse. He cackles and runs down the steps. At the corner of the house, he stops and turns.*

Baby, you keep Mr. Vicarro comfo'table while I'm ginnin' out that twenty-seven wagons full of cotton. Th' good neighbor policy, Mr. Vicarro. You do me a good turn an' I'll do you a good one! Be see'n' yuh! So long, Baby!

*He walks away with an energetic stride.*

VICARRO:

The good neighbor policy!

*He sits on the porch steps.*

FLORA:

(*Sitting on the swing*)

Izzen he out-*ray*-juss!

*She laughs foolishly and puts the purse in her lap. VI-
CARRO stares gloomily across the dancing brilliance of
the fields. His lip sticks out like a pouting child's. A
rooster crows in the distance.*

FLORA:

I would'n' dare to expose myself like that.

VICARRO:

Expose? To what?

FLORA:

The sun. I take a terrible burn. I'll never forget the
burn I took one time. It was on Moon Lake one Sunday
before I was married. I never did like t' go fishin' but
this young fellow, one of the Peterson boys, insisted that
we go fishin'. Well, he didn't catch nothin' but jes' kep'
fishin' an' fishin' an' I set there in th' boat with all that
hot sun on me. I said, Stay under the willows. But he
would'n' lissen to me, an' sure enough I took such an
awful burn I had t' sleep on m' stummick th' nex' three
nights.

VICARRO:

(*Absently*)

What did you say? You got sunburned?

FLORA:

Yes. One time on Moon Lake.

*Page 160*

VICARRO:

That's too bad. You got over it all right?

FLORA:

Oh, yes. Finally. Yes.

VICARRO:

That must 've been pretty bad.

FLORA:

I fell in the lake once, too. Also with one of the Peterson boys. On another fishing trip. That was a wild bunch of boys, those Peterson boys. I never went out with 'em but something happened which made me wish I hadn't. One time, sunburned. One time, nearly drowned. One time—poison ivy! Well, lookin' back on it, now, we had a good deal of fun in spite of it, though.

VICARRO:

The good neighbor policy, huh?

*He slaps his boot with the riding crop. Then he rises from steps.*

FLORA:

You might as well come up on th' po'ch an' make you'-self as comfo'table as you can.

VICARRO:

Uh-huh.

FLORA:

I'm not much good at—makin' conversation.

VICARRO:

(*Finally noticing her*)

Now don't you bother to make conversation for my benefit, Mrs. Meighan. I'm the type that prefers a quiet understanding.

FLORA *laughs uncertainly.*

One thing I always notice about you ladies . . .

FLORA:

What's that, Mr. Vicarro?

VICARRO:

You always have something in your hands—to hold onto. Now that kid purse . . .

FLORA:

My purse?

VICARRO:

You have no reason to keep that purse in your hands. You're certainly not afraid that I'm going to snatch it!

FLORA:

Oh, God, no! I wassen afraid of that!

VICARRO:

That wouldn't be the good neighbor policy, would it? But you hold onto that purse because it gives you something to get a grip on. Isn't that right?

FLORA:

Yes. I always like to have something in my hands.

VICARRO:

Sure you do. You feel what a lot of uncertain things there are. Gins burn down. The volunteer fire department don't have decent equipment. Nothing is any protection. The afternoon sun is hot. It's no protection. The trees are back of the house. They're no protection. The goods that dress is made of—is no protection. So what do you do, Mrs. Meighan? You pick up the white kid purse. It's solid. It's sure. It's certain. It's something to hold *on* to. You get what I mean?

FLORA:

Yeah. I think I do.

VICARRO:

It gives you a feeling of being attached to something. The mother protects the baby? No, no, no—the baby protects the mother! From being lost and empty and having nothing but lifeless things in her hands! Maybe you think there isn't much connection!

FLORA:

You'll have to excuse me from thinking. I'm too lazy.

VICARRO:

What's your name, Mrs. Meighan?

FLORA:

Flora.

VICARRO:

Mine is Silva. Something not gold but—Silva!

FLORA:

Like a silver dollar?

VICARRO:

No, like a silver dime! It's an Italian name. I'm a native of New Orleans.

FLORA:

Then it's not sunburn. You're natcherally dark.

VICARRO:

(*Raising his undershirt from his belly*)
Look at this!

FLORA:

Mr. Vicarro!

VICARRO:

Just as dark as my arm is!

FLORA:

You don't have to show me! I'm not from Missouri!

VICARRO:

(*Grinning*)

Excuse me.

FLORA:

(*She laughs nervously*)

Whew! I'm sorry to say we don't have a coke in the house. We meant to get a case of cokes las' night, but what with all the excitement going on—

VICARRO:

What excitement was that?

FLORA:

Oh, the fire and all.

VICARRO:

(*Lighting a cigarette*)

I shouldn't think you all would of been excited about the fire.

FLORA:

A fire is always exciting. After a fire, dogs an' chickens don't sleep. I don't think our chickens got to sleep all night.

VICARRO:

No?

FLORA:

They cackled an' fussed an' flopped around on the roost —took on something awful! Myself, I couldn't sleep either. I jus' lay there an' sweated all night long.

VICARRO:

On account of th' fire?

FLORA:

An' the heat an' mosquitoes. And I was mad at Jake.

VICARRO:

Mad at Mr. Meighan? What about?

FLORA:

Oh, he went off an' left me settin' here on this ole po'ch last night without a Coca-Cola on the place.

VICARRO:

Went off an' left you, did he?

FLORA:

Yep. Right after supper. An' when he got back the fire 'd already broke out an' instead of drivin' in to town like he said, he decided to go an' take a look at your burnt-down cotton gin. I got smoke in my eyes an' my nose an' throat. It hurt my sinus an' I was in such a wo'n-out, nervous condition, it made me cry. I cried like a baby. Finally took two teaspoons of paregoric. Enough to put an elephant to sleep. But still I stayed awake an' heard them chickens carryin' on out there!

VICARRO:

It sounds like you passed a very uncomfortable night.

FLORA:

Sounds like? Well, it *was*.

VICARRO:

So Mr. Meighan—you say—disappeared after supper? *There is a pause while* FLORA *looks at him blankly.*

FLORA:

Huh?

VICARRO:

You say Mr. Meighan was out of the house for a while after supper?

*Something in his tone makes her aware of her indis-
cretion.*

FLORA:

Oh—uh—just for a moment.

VICARRO:

Just for a moment, huh? How long a moment?
*He stares at her very hard.*

FLORA:

What are you driving at, Mr. Vicarro?

VICARRO:

Driving at? Nothing.

FLORA:

You're looking at me so funny.

VICARRO:

He disappeared for a moment! Is that what he did?
How long a moment did he disappear for? Can you
remember, Mrs. Meighan?

FLORA:

What difference does that make? What's it to you,
anyhow?

VICARRO:

Why should you mind me asking?

FLORA:

You make this sound like I was on trial for something!

VICARRO:

Don't you like to pretend like you're a witness?

FLORA:

Witness of what, Mr. Vicarro?

VICARRO:

Why—for instance—say—a case of arson!

FLORA:

(*Wetting her lips*)

Case of—? What is—arson?

VICARRO:

The willful destruction of property by fire.

*He slaps his boots sharply with the riding crop.*

FLORA:

(*Startled*)

Oh!

*She nervously fingers the purse.*

Well, now, don't you go and be getting any—funny ideas.

VICARRO:

Ideas about what, Mrs. Meighan?

FLORA:

My husband's disappearin'—after supper. I can explain that.

VICARRO:

Can you?

FLORA:

Sure I can.

VICARRO:

Good! How do you explain it?

*He stares at her. She looks down.*

What's the matter? Can't you collect your thoughts, Mrs. Meighan?

FLORA:

No, but—

VICARRO:

Your mind's a blank on the subject?

FLORA:

Look here, now—

*She squirms on the swing.*

VICARRO:

You find it impossible to remember just what your husband disappeared for after supper? You can't imagine what kind of errand it was that he went out on, can you?

FLORA:

No! No, I can't!

VICARRO:

But when he returned—let's see . . . the fire had just broken out at the Syndicate Plantation?

FLORA:

Mr. Vicarro, I don't have the slightest idear what you could be driving at.

VICARRO:

You're a very unsatisfactory witness, Mrs. Meighan.

FLORA:

I never can think when people—stare straight at me.

VICARRO:

Okay. I'll look away, then.

*He turns his back to her.*

Now does that improve your memory any? Now are you able to concentrate on the question?

FLORA:

Huh . . .

VICARRO:

No? You're not?

*He turns around again, grinning evilly.*

Well . . . shall we drop the subject?

FLORA:

I sure do wish you would.

VICARRO:

It's no use crying over a burnt-down gin. This world is built on the principle of tit for tat.

FLORA:

What do you mean?

VICARRO:

Nothing at all specific. Mind if I . . . ?

FLORA:

What?

VICARRO:

You want to move over a little an' make some room? FLORA *edges aside on the swing. He sits down with her.* I like a swing. I've always liked to sit an' rock on a swing. Relaxes you. . . . You relaxed?

FLORA:

Sure.

VICARRO:

No, you're not. Your nerves are all tied up.

FLORA:

Well, you made me feel kind of nervous. All of them questions you ast me about the fire.

VICARRO:

I didn' ask you questions about the fire. I only asked you about your husband's leaving the house after supper.

FLORA:

I explained that to you.

VICARRO:

Sure. That's right. You did. The good neighbor policy.

*Page 169*

That was a lovely remark your husband made about the good neighbor policy. I see what he means by that now.

FLORA:

He was thinking about President Roosevelt's speech. We sat up an' lissened to it one night last week.

VICARRO:

No, I think that he was talking about something closer to home, Mrs. Meighan. You do me a good turn and I'll do you one, that was the way that he put it. You have a piece of cotton on your face. Hold still—I'll pick it off.

*He delicately removes the lint.*

There now.

FLORA:

(*Nervously*)

Thanks.

VICARRO:

There's a lot of fine cotton lint floating round in the air.

FLORA:

I know there is. It irritates my nose. I think it gets up in my sinus.

VICARRO:

Well, you're a delicate woman.

FLORA:

Delicate? Me? Oh, no. I'm too big for that.

VICARRO:

Your size is part of your delicacy, Mrs. Meighan.

FLORA:

How do you mean?

VICARRO:

There's a lot of you, but every bit of you is delicate.

Choice. Delectable, I might say.

FLORA:

Huh?

VICARRO:

I mean you're altogether lacking in any—coarseness.
You're soft. Fine fibered. And smooth.

FLORA:

Our talk is certainly taking a personal turn.

VICARRO:

Yes. You make me think of cotton.

FLORA:

Huh?

VICARRO:

Cotton!

FLORA:

Well! Should I say thanks or something?

VICARRO:

No, just smile, Mrs. Meighan. You have an attractive
smile. Dimples!

FLORA:

No . . .

VICARRO:

Yes, you have! Smile, Mrs. Meighan! Come on—smile!
FLORA *averts her face, smiling helplessly.*
There now. See? You've got them!
*He delicately touches one of the dimples.*

FLORA:

Please don't touch me. I don't like to be touched.

VICARRO:

Then why do you giggle?

FLORA:

Can't help it. You make me feel kind of hysterical, Mr. Vicarro. Mr. Vicarro—

VICARRO:

Yes?

FLORA:

I hope you don't think that Jake was mixed up in that fire. I swear to goodness he never left the front porch. I remember it perfeckly now. We just set here on the swing till the fire broke out and then we drove in town.

VICARRO:

To celebrate?

FLORA:

No, no, no.

VICARRO:

Twenty-seven wagons full of cotton's a pretty big piece of business to fall in your lap like a gift from the gods, Mrs. Meighan.

FLORA:

I thought you said that we would drop the subjeck.

VICARRO:

You brought it up that time.

FLORA:

Well, please don't try to mix me up any more. I swear to goodness the fire had already broke out when he got back.

VICARRO:

That's not what you told me a moment ago.

FLORA:

You got me all twisted up. We went in town. The fire broke out an' we didn't know about it.

VICARRO:

I thought you said it irritated your sinus.

FLORA:

Oh, my God, you sure put words in my mouth. Maybe I'd better make us some lemonade.

VICARRO:

Don't go to the trouble.

FLORA:

I'll go in an' fix it direckly, but right at this moment I'm too weak to get up. I don't know why, but I can't hardly hold my eyes open. They keep falling shut. . . . I think it's a little too crowded, two on a swing. Will you do me a favor an' set back down over there?

VICARRO:

Why do you want me to move?

FLORA:

It makes too much body heat when we're crowded together.

VICARRO:

One body can borrow coolness from another.

FLORA:

I always heard that bodies borrowed heat.

VICARRO:

Not in this case. I'm cool.

FLORA:

You don't seem like it to me.

VICARRO:

I'm just as cool as a cucumber. If you don't believe it, touch me.

FLORA:

Where?

VICARRO:

Anywhere.

FLORA:

(*Rising with great effort*)

Excuse me. I got to go in.

*He pulls her back down.*

What did you do that for?

VICARRO:

I don't want to be deprived of your company yet.

FLORA:

Mr. Vicarro, you're getting awf'ly familiar.

VICARRO:

Haven't you got any fun-loving spirit about you?

FLORA:

This isn't fun.

VICARRO:

Then why do you giggle?

FLORA:

I'm ticklish! Quit switching me, will yuh?

VICARRO:

I'm just shooing the flies off.

FLORA:

Leave 'em be, then, please. They don't hurt nothin'.

VICARRO:

. I think you like to be switched.

FLORA:

I don't. I wish you'd quit.

VICARRO:

You'd like to be switched harder.

FLORA:

No, I wouldn't.

VICARRO:

That blue mark on your wrist—

FLORA:

What about it?

VICARRO:

I've got a suspicion.

FLORA:

Of what?

VICARRO:

It was twisted. By your husband.

FLORA:

You're crazy.

VICARRO:

Yes, it was. And you liked it.

FLORA:

I certainly didn't. Would you mind moving your arm?

VICARRO:

Don't be so skittish.

FLORA:

Awright. I'll get up then.

VICARRO:

Go on.

FLORA:

I feel so weak.

VICARRO:

Dizzy?

FLORA:

A little bit. Yeah. My head's spinning round. I wish you would stop the swing.

VICARRO:

It's not swinging much.

FLORA:

But even a little's too much.

VICARRO:

You're a delicate woman. A pretty big woman, too.

FLORA:

So is America. Big.

VICARRO:

That's a funny remark.

FLORA:

Yeah. I don't know why I made it. My head's so buzzy.

VICARRO:

Fuzzy?

FLORA:

Fuzzy an'—buzzy. . . . Is something on my arm?

VICARRO:

No.

FLORA:

Then what 're you brushing?

VICARRO:

Sweat off.

FLORA:

Leave it alone.

VICARRO:

Let me wipe it.

*He brushes her arm with a handkerchief.*

FLORA:

(*Laughing weakly*)
No, please, don't. It feels funny.

VICARRO:

How does it feel?

FLORA:

It tickles me. All up an' down. You cut it out now. If you don't cut it out I'm going to call.

VICARRO:

Call who?

FLORA:

I'm going to call that nigger. The nigger that's cutting the grass across the road.

VICARRO:

Go on. Call, then.

FLORA:

(*Weakly*)
Hey! Hey, boy!

VICARRO:

Can't you call any louder?

FLORA:

I feel so funny. What is the matter with me?

VICARRO:

You're just relaxing. You're big. A big type of woman. I like you. Don't get so excited.

FLORA:

I'm not, but you—

VICARRO:

What am I doing?

FLORA:

Suspicions. About my husband and ideas you have about me.

VICARRO:

Such as what?

FLORA:

He burnt your gin down. He didn't. And I'm not a big piece of cotton.

*She pulls herself up.*

I'm going inside.

VICARRO:

(*Rising*)

I think that's a good idea.

FLORA:

I said I was. Not you.

VICARRO:

Why not me?

FLORA:

Inside it might be crowded, with you an' me.

VICARRO:

Three's a crowd. We're two.

FLORA:

You stay out. Wait here.

VICARRO:

What'll you do?

FLORA:

I'll make us a pitcher of nice cold lemonade.

VICARRO:

Okay. You go on in.

FLORA:

What'll you do?

VICARRO:

I'll follow.

FLORA:

That's what I figured you might be aiming to do. We'll both stay out.

*Page 178*

VICARRO:

In the sun?

FLORA:

We'll sit back down in th' shade.

*He blocks her.*

Don't stand in my way.

VICARRO:

You're standing in mine.

FLORA:

I'm dizzy.

VICARRO:

You ought to lie down.

FLORA:

How can I?

VICARRO:

Go in.

FLORA:

You'd follow me.

VICARRO:

What if I did?

FLORA:

I'm afraid.

VICARRO:

You're starting to cry.

FLORA:

I'm afraid!

VICARRO:

What of?

FLORA:

Of you.

VICARRO:

I'm little.

FLORA:

I'm dizzy. My knees are so weak they're like water. I've got to sit down.

VICARRO:

Go in.

FLORA:

I can't.

VICARRO:

Why not?

FLORA:

You'd follow.

VICARRO:

Would that be so awful?

FLORA:

You've got a mean look in your eyes and I don't like the whip. Honest to God, he never. He didn't, I swear!

VICARRO:

Do what?

FLORA:

The fire . . .

VICARRO:

Go on.

FLORA:

Please don't!

VICARRO:

Don't what?

FLORA:

Put it down. The whip, please put it down. Leave it out here on the porch.

*Page 180*

VICARRO:

What are you scared of?

FLORA:

You.

VICARRO:

Go on.

*She turns helplessly and moves to the screen. He pulls it open.*

FLORA:

Don't follow. Please don't follow!

*She sways uncertainly. He presses his hand against her. She moves inside. He follows. The door is shut quietly. The gin pumps slowly and steadily across the road. From inside the house there is a wild and despairing cry. A door is slammed. The cry is repeated more faintly.*

## Scene III

*It is about nine o'clock the same evening. Although the sky behind the house is a dusky rose color, a full September moon of almost garish intensity gives the front of the house a ghostly brilliance. Dogs are howling like demons across the prostrate fields of the Delta.*

*The front porch of the Meighans is empty. After a moment the screen door is pushed slowly open and Flora Meighan emerges gradually. Her appearance is ravaged. Her eyes have a vacant limpidity in the moonlight, her lips are slightly apart. She moves with her hands stretched gropingly before her till she has reached a pillar of the porch. There she stops and stands moan-*

*ing a little. Her hair hangs loose and disordered. The*
*upper part of her body is unclothed except for a torn*
*pink band about her breasts. Dark streaks are visible on*
*the bare shoulders and arms and there is a large dis-*
*coloration along one cheek. A dark trickle, now con-*
*gealed, descends from one corner of her mouth. These*
*more apparent tokens she covers with one hand when*
JAKE *comes up on the porch. He is now heard approach-*
*ing, singing to himself.*

JAKE:

By the light—by the light—by the light—Of the sil-very
mo-o-on!

*Instinctively* FLORA *draws back into the sharply etched*
*shadows from the porch roof.* JAKE *is too tired and tri-*
*umphant to notice her appearance.*

How's a baby?

FLORA *utters a moaning grunt.*

Tired? Too tired t' talk? Well, that's how I feel. Too
tired t' talk. Too goddam tired t' speak a friggin' word!
*He lets himself down on the steps, groaning and with-*
*out giving* FLORA *more than a glance.*

Twenty-seven wagons full of cotton. That's how much
I've ginned since ten this mawnin'. A man-size job.

FLORA:

(*Huskily*)
Uh-huh. . . . A man-size—job. . . .

JAKE:

*Twen*-ty *sev*-en *wa*-gons *full of cot*-ton!

FLORA:

(*Senselessly repeating*)
*Twen*-ty *sev*-en *wa*-gons *full* of *cot*-ton!

*A dog howls.* FLORA *utters a breathless laugh.*

JAKE:

What're you laughin' at, honey? Not at me, I hope.

FLORA:

No. . . .

JAKE:

That's good. The job that I've turned out is nothing to laugh at. I drove that pack of niggers like a mule-skinner. They don't have a brain in their bodies. All they got is bodies. You got to drive, drive, drive. I don't even see how niggers eat without somebody to tell them to put the food in their moufs!
*She laughs again, like water spilling out of her mouth.*
Huh! You got a laugh like a—! Christ, a terrific day's work I finished.

FLORA:

(*Slowly*)
I would'n' brag—about it. . . .

JAKE:

I'm not braggin' about it, I'm just sayin' I done a big day's work, I'm all wo'n out an' I want a little appreciation, not cross speeches. Honey . . .

FLORA:

I'm not—
*She laughs again.*
—makin' cross speeches.

JAKE:

To take on a big piece of work an' finish it up an' mention the fack that it's finished I wouldn't call braggin'.

FLORA:

You're not the only one's—done a big day's—work.

JAKE:

Who else that you know of?

*There is a pause.*

FLORA:

Maybe you think that I had an easy time.

*Her laughter spills out again.*

JAKE:

You're laughin' like you been on a goddam jag.

FLORA *laughs.*

What did you get pissed on? Roach poison or citronella? I think I make it pretty easy for you, workin' like a mule-skinner so you can hire you a nigger to do the wash an' take the housework on. An elephant woman who acks as frail as a kitten, that's the kind of a woman I got on m' hands.

FLORA:

Sure. . . .

*She laughs.*

You make it easy!

JAKE:

I've yet t' see you lift a little finger. Even gotten too lazy t' put you' things on. Round the house ha'f naked all th' time. Y' live in a cloud. All you can think of is "Give me a Coca-Cola!" Well, you better look out. They got a new bureau in the guvamint files. It's called U.W. Stands for Useless Wimmen. Tha's secret plans on foot t' have 'em shot!

*He laughs at his joke.*

FLORA:

Secret—plans—on foot?

JAKE:

T' have 'em *shot*.

FLORA:

That's good. I'm glad t' hear it.

*She laughs again.*

JAKE:

I come home tired an' you cain't wait t' peck at me.
What're you cross about now?

FLORA:

I think it was a mistake.

JAKE:

What was a mistake?

FLORA:

Fo' you t' fool with th' Syndicate—Plantation. . . .

JAKE:

I don't know about that. We wuh kind of up against it,
honey. Th' Syndicate buyin' up all th' lan' aroun' here
an' turnin' the ole croppers off it without their wages—
mighty near busted ev'ry mercantile store in Two Rivers
County! An' then they build their own gin to gin their
own cotton. It looked for a while like I was stuck up
high an' dry. But when the gin burnt down an' Mr.
Vicarro decided he'd better throw a little bus'ness my
way—I'd say the situation was much improved!

FLORA:

(*She laughs weakly*)

Then maybe you don't understand th' good neighbor—
policy.

JAKE:

Don't understand it? Why, I'm the boy that invented it.

FLORA:

Huh-huh! What an—*invention!* All I can say is—I hope you're satisfied now that you've ginned out—twenty-seven wagons full of—cotton.

JAKE:

Vicarro was pretty well pleased we'en he dropped over.

FLORA:

Yeah. He was—pretty well—pleased.

JAKE:

How did you all get along?

FLORA:

We got along jus' fine. Jus' fine an'—dandy.

JAKE:

He didn't seem like a such a bad little guy. He takes a sensible attitude.

FLORA:

(*Laughing helplessly*)

He—sure—does!

JAKE:

I hope you made him comfo'table in the house?

FLORA:

(*Giggling*)

I made him a pitcher—of nice cold—lemonade!

JAKE:

With a little gin in it, huh? That's how you got pissed. A nice cool drink don't sound bad to me right now. Got any left?

FLORA:

Not a bit, Mr. Meighan. We drank it *a-a-ll* up!

*She flops onto the swing.*

JAKE:

So you didn't have such a tiresome time after all?

FLORA:

No. Not tiresome a bit. I had a nice conversation with Mistuh—Vicarro. . . .

JAKE:

What did you all talk about?

FLORA:

Th' good neighbor policy.

JAKE:

(*Chuckling*)

How does he feel about th' good neighbor policy?

FLORA:

Oh—

*She giggles.*

He thinks it's a—good idea! He says—

JAKE:

Huh?

FLORA *laughs weakly.*

Says what?

FLORA:

Says—

*She goes off into another spasm of laughter.*

JAKE:

What ever he said must've been a panic!

FLORA:

He says—

*Controlling her spasm.*

—he don't think he'll build him a new cotton gin any more. He's gonna let you do a-a-lll his ginnin'—fo' him!

JAKE:

I told you he'd take a sensible attitude.

FLORA:

Yeah. Tomorrow he plans t' come back—with lots more cotton. Maybe another twenty-seven wagons.

JAKE:

Yeah?

FLORA:

An' while you're ginnin' it out—he'll have me entertain him with—nice lemonade!

*She has another fit of giggles.*

JAKE:

The more I hear about that lemonade the better I like it. Lemonade highballs, huh? Mr. Thomas Collins?

FLORA:

I guess it's—gonna go on fo'—th' rest of th'—summer. . . .

JAKE:

(*Rising and stretching happily*)

Well, it'll . . . it'll soon be fall. Cooler nights comin' on.

FLORA:

I don't know that that will put a—stop to it—though. . . .

JAKE:

(*Obliviously*)

The air feels cooler already. You shouldn't be settin' out here without you' shirt on, honey. A change in the air can give you a mighty bad cold.

FLORA:

I couldn't stan' nothin' on me—nex' to my—skin.

JAKE:

It ain't the heat that gives you all them hives, it's too much liquor. Grog blossoms, that's what you got! I'm goin' inside to the toilet. When I come out—

*He opens the screen door and goes in.*

—We'll drive in town an' see what's at th' movies. You go hop in the Chevy!

FLORA *laughs to herself. She slowly opens the huge kid purse and removes a wad of Kleenex. She touches herself tenderly here and there, giggling breathlessly.*

FLORA:

(*Aloud*)

I really oughtn' t' have a white kid purse. It's wadded full of—Kleenex—to make it big—like a baby! Big—in my arms—like a baby!

JAKE:

(*From inside*)

What did you say, baby?

FLORA:

(*Dragging herself up by the chain of the swing*)

I'm not—baby. Mama! Ma! That's—me. . . .

*Cradling the big white purse in her arms, she advances slowly and tenderly to the edge of the porch. The moon shines full on her smiling and ravaged face. She begins to rock and sway gently, rocking the purse in her arms and crooning.*

Rock-a-bye baby—in uh tree-tops!

If a wind blows—a cradle will rock!

*She descends a step.*

If a bough bends—a baby will fall!

*She descends another step.*

Down will come baby—cradle—an'—all!

*She laughs and stares raptly and vacantly up at the moon.*

# The Long Stay Cut Short

## OR

# The Unsatisfactory Supper

### THE CHARACTERS

BABY DOLL

ARCHIE LEE

AUNT ROSE

*The curtain rises on the porch and side yard of a shotgun cottage in Blue Mountain, Mississippi. The frame house is faded and has a greenish-gray cast with dark streaks from the roof, and there are irregularities in the lines of the building. Behind it the dusky cyclorama is stained with the rose of sunset, which is stormy-looking, and the wind has a catlike whine.*

*Upstage from the porch, in the center of the side yard, is a very large rose bush, the beauty of which is somehow sinister-looking.*

*A Prokofiev sort of music introduces the scene and sets a mood of grotesque lyricism.*

*The screen door opens with a snarl of rusty springs and latches: this stops the music.*

MRS. "BABY DOLL" BOWMAN *appears. She is a large and*

*indolent woman, but her amplitude is not benign, her stu-
pidity is not comfortable. There is a suggestion of Egypt
in the arrangement of her glossy black hair and the purple
linen dress and heavy brass jewelry that she is wearing.*

ARCHIE LEE BOWMAN *comes out and sucks at his teeth.
He is a large man with an unhealthy, chalk-white face
and slack figure.*

(*The evenly cadenced lines of the dialogue between* BABY
DOLL *and* ARCHIE LEE *may be given a singsong reading,
somewhat like a grotesque choral incantation, and passages
may be divided as strophe and antistrophe by* BABY DOLL'S
*movements back and forth on the porch.*)

ARCHIE LEE:

The old lady used to could set a right fair table, but
not any more. The food has fallen off bad around here
lately.

BABY DOLL:

You're right about that, Archie Lee. I can't argue with
you.

ARCHIE LEE:

A good mess of greens is a satisfactory meal if it's
cooked with salt pork an' left on th' stove till it's tender,
but thrown in a platter ha'f cooked an' unflavored, it
ain't even fit for hog-slops.

BABY DOLL:

It's hard t' spoil greens but the old lady sure did spoil
'em.

ARCHIE LEE:

How did she manage t' do it?

*Page 192*

BABY DOLL:

(*Slowly and contemptuously*)

Well, she had 'em on th' stove for about an hour. Said she thought they wuh boilin'. I went in the kitchen. The stove was stone cold. The silly old thing had forgotten to build a fire in it. So I called her back. I said, "Aunt Rose, I think I understand why the greens aren't boilin'." "Why aren't they boilin'?" she says. "Well," I told her, "it might have something to do with the fack that the stove issen lighted!"

ARCHIE LEE:

What did she say about that?

BABY DOLL:

Juss threw back her head an' cackled. "Why, I thought my stove was lighted," she said. "I thought my greens wuh boilin'." Everything is *my*. My stove, my greens, my kitchen. She has taken possession of everything on the place.

ARCHIE LEE:

She's getting delusions of grandeur.

*A high, thin laugh is heard inside.*

Why does she cackle that way?

BABY DOLL:

How should I know why she cackles! I guess it's supposed to show that she's in a good humor.

ARCHIE LEE:

A thing like that can become awf'ly aggravating.

BABY DOLL:

It gets on my nerves so bad I could haul off and scream. And obstinate! She's just as obstinate as a mule.

ARCHIE LEE:

A person can be obstinate and still cook greens.

BABY DOLL:

Not if they're so obstinate they won't even look in a stove t' see if it's lighted.

ARCHIE LEE:

Why don't you keep the old lady out of the kitchen?

BABY DOLL:

You get me a nigger and I'll keep her out of the kitchen. *The screen door creaks open and* AUNT ROSE *comes out on the porch. She is breathless with the exertion of moving from the kitchen, and clings to a porch column while she is catching her breath. She is the type of old lady, about eighty-five years old, that resembles a delicate white-headed monkey. She has on a dress of gray calico which has become too large for her shrunken figure. She has a continual fluttering in her chest which makes her laugh in a witless manner. Neither of the pair on the porch pays any apparent attention to her, though she nods and smiles brightly at each.*

AUNT ROSE:

I brought out m' scissors. Tomorrow is Sunday an' I can't stand for my house to be without flowers on Sunday. Besides, if we don't cut the roses the wind'll just blow them away.

BABY DOLL:

(*Yawns ostentatiously.* ARCHIE LEE *sucks loudly at his teeth.* BABY DOLL, *venting her irritation*)

Will you quit suckin' your teeth?

ARCHIE LEE:

I got something stuck in my teeth an' I can't remove it.

BABY DOLL:

There's such a thing as a toothpick made for that purpose.

ARCHIE LEE:

I told you at breakfast we didn't have any toothpicks. I told you the same thing at lunch and the same thing at supper. Does it have to appear in the paper for you to believe it?

BABY DOLL:

There's other things with a point besides a toothpick.

AUNT ROSE:

(*Excitedly*)

Archie Lee, son!

*She produces a spool of thread from her bulging skirt pocket.*

You bite off a piece of this thread and run it between your teeth and if that don't dislodge a morsel nothing else will!

ARCHIE LEE:

(*Slamming his feet from porch rail to floor*)

Now listen, you all, I want you both to get this. If I want to suck at my teeth, I'm going to suck at my teeth!

AUNT ROSE:

That's right, Archie Lee, you go on and suck at your teeth as much as you want to.

BABY DOLL *grunts disgustedly.* ARCHIE LEE *throws his feet back on the rail and goes on sucking his teeth loudly.*

AUNT ROSE:

(*Hesitantly*)

Archie Lee, son, you weren't satisfied with your supper. I noticed you left a lot of greens on your plate.

ARCHIE LEE:

I'm not strong on greens.

AUNT ROSE:

I'm surprised to hear you say that.

ARCHIE LEE:

I don't see why you should be. As far as I know I never declared any terrible fondness for greens in your presence, Aunt Rose.

AUNT ROSE:

Well, somebody did.

ARCHIE LEE:

Somebody probably did sometime and somewhere but that don't mean it was me.

AUNT ROSE:

(*With a nervous laugh*)

Baby Doll, who is it dotes on greens so much?

BABY DOLL:

(*Wearily*)

I don't know who dotes on greens, Aunt Rose.

AUNT ROSE:

All these likes and dislikes, it's hard to keep straight in your head. But Archie Lee's easy t' cook for, yes, he is, easy t' cook for! Jim's a complainer, oh, my what a complainer. And Susie's household! What complainers! Every living one of them's a complainer! They're such complainers I die of nervous prostration when I'm cooking for them. But Archie Lee, here, he takes whatever you give him an' seems to love ev'ry bite of it!
*She touches his head.*
Bless you, honey, for being so easy t' cook for!

ARCHIE LEE *picks up his chair and moves it roughly away.*

AUNT ROSE:

(*She laughs nervously and digs in her capacious pocket for the scissors.*)

Now I'm goin' down there an' clip a few roses befo' th' wind blows 'em away 'cause I can't stand my house to be without flowers on Sunday. An' soon as I've finished with that, I'm goin' back in my kitchen an' light up my stove an' cook you some eggs Birmingham. I won't have my men-folks unsatisfied with their supper. Won't have it, I won't stand for it!

*She gets to the bottom of the steps and pauses for breath.*

ARCHIE LEE:

What is eggs Birmingham?

AUNT ROSE:

Why, eggs Birmingham was Baby Doll's daddy's pet dish.

ARCHIE LEE:

That don't answer my question.

AUNT ROSE:

(*As though confiding a secret*)

I'll tell you how to prepare them.

ARCHIE LEE:

I don't care how you prepare them, I just want to know what they are.

AUNT ROSE:

(*Reasonably*)

Well, son, I can't say what they are without telling how to prepare them. You cut some bread slices and take the centers out of them. You put the bread slices in a skillet with butter. Then into each cut-out center you drop one egg and on top of the eggs you put the cut-out centers.

ARCHIE LEE:

(*Sarcastically*)

Do you build a fire in th' stove?

BABY DOLL:

No, you forget to do that. That's why they call them eggs Birmingham, I suppose.

*She laughs at her wit.*

AUNT ROSE:

(*Vivaciously*)

That's what they call them, they call them eggs Birmingham and Baby Doll's daddy was just insane about them. When Baby Doll's daddy was not satisfied with his supper, he'd call for eggs Birmingham and would stomp his feet on the floor until I'd fixed 'em!

*This recollection seems to amuse her so that she nearly falls over.*

He'd stomp his feet on th' floor!—until I'd fixed 'em. . . .

*Her laughter dies out and she wanders away from the porch, examining the scissors.*

BABY DOLL:

That old woman is going out of her mind.

ARCHIE LEE:

How long is she been with us?

BABY DOLL:

She come in October.

ARCHIE LEE:

No, it was August. She pulled in here last August.

BABY DOLL:

Was it in August? Yes, it was, it was August.

ARCHIE LEE:

Why don't she go an' cackle at Susie's awhile?

BABY DOLL:

Susie don't have a bed for her.

ARCHIE LEE:

Then how about Jim?

BABY DOLL:

She was at Jim's direckly before she came here and Jim's wife said she stole from her and that's why she left.

ARCHIE LEE:

I don't believe she stole from her. Do you believe she stole from her?

BABY DOLL:

I don't believe she stole from her. I think it was just an excuse to get rid of her.

AUNT ROSE *has arrived at the rose bush. The wind comes up and nearly blows her off her feet. She staggers around and laughs at her precarious balance.*

AUNT ROSE:

Oh, my gracious! Ha-ha! Oh! Ha-ha-ha!

BABY DOLL:

Why, every time I lay my pocketbook down, the silly old thing picks it up and comes creeping in to me with it, and says, "Count the change."

ARCHIE LEE:

What does she do that for?

BABY DOLL:

She's afraid I'll accuse her of stealing like Jim's wife did.

AUNT ROSE:

    (*Singing to herself as she creeps around the rose bush*)
            Rock of Ages, cleft for me,
            Let me hide myself in thee!

ARCHIE LEE:

    Your buck-toothed cousin named Bunny, didn't he hit
on a new way of using oil waste?

BABY DOLL:

    He did an' he didn't.

ARCHIE LEE:

    That statement don't make sense.

BABY DOLL:

    Well, you know Bunny. He hits on something and ropes
in a few stockholders and then it blows up and the
stockholders all go to court. And also he says that his
wife's got female trouble.

ARCHIE LEE:

    They've all got something because they're not mental
giants but they've got enough sense to know the old
lady is going to break down pretty soon and none of
'em wants it to be while she's on their hands.

BABY DOLL:

    That is about the size of it.

ARCHIE LEE:

    And I'm stuck with her?

BABY DOLL:

    Don't holler.

ARCHIE LEE:

    I'm nominated the goat!

BABY DOLL:

    Don't holler, don't holler!

*Page 200*

AUNT ROSE *sings faintly by rose bush*.

ARCHIE LEE:

Then pass the old lady on to one of them others.

BABY DOLL:

Which one, Archie Lee?

ARCHIE LEE:

Eeeny-meeny-miney-mo. —Mo gets her.

BABY DOLL:

Which is "Mo"?

ARCHIE LEE:

Not me!

*Moving slowly and cautiously around the rose bush with her scissors,* AUNT ROSE *sings to herself. Intersperses lines of the hymn with dialogue on porch. A blue dusk is gathering in the yard but a pool of clear light remains upon the rose bush.*

ARCHIE LEE:

(*With religious awe*)

Some of them get these lingering types of diseases and have to be given morphine, and they tell me that morphine is just as high as a cat's back.

BABY DOLL:

Some of them hang on forever, taking morphine.

ARCHIE LEE:

And quantities of it!

BABY DOLL:

Yes, they take quantities of it!

ARCHIE LEE:

Suppose the old lady broke a hipbone or something, something that called for morphine!

BABY DOLL:

The rest of the folks would have to pitch in and help us.

ARCHIE LEE:

Try and extract a dime from your brother Jim! Or Susie or Tom or Bunny! They're all tight as drums, they squeeze ev'ry nickel until th' buffalo bleeds!

BABY DOLL:

They don't have much and what they have they hold onto.

ARCHIE LEE:

Well, if she does, if she breaks down an' dies on us here, I'm giving you fair warning—

*Lurches heavily to his feet and spits over edge of porch.*

I'll have her burned up and her ashes put in an old Coca-Cola bottle—

*Flops down again.*

Unless your folks kick in with the price of a coffin!

AUNT ROSE *has clipped a few roses. Now she wanders toward the front of the cottage with them.*

Here she comes back. Now tell her.

BABY DOLL:

Tell her what?

ARCHIE LEE:

That she's outstayed her welcome.

AUNT ROSE:

(*Still at some distance*)

I want you children to look.

ARCHIE LEE:

You going to tell her?

AUNT ROSE:

I want you children to look at these poems of nature!

ARCHIE LEE:

Or do I have to tell her?

BABY DOLL:

You hush up and I'll tell her.

ARCHIE LEE:

Then tell her right now, and no more pussyfooting.

AUNT ROSE:

(*Now close to the porch*)

Look at them, look at them, children, they're poems of nature!

*But the "Children" stare unresponsively, not at the flowers but at* AUNT ROSE's *face with its extravagant brightness. She laughs uncertainly and turns to* ARCHIE LEE *for a more direct appeal.*

Archie Lee, aren't they, aren't they just poems of nature?

*He grunts and gets up, and as he passes* BABY DOLL's *chair he gives it a kick to remind her.* BABY DOLL *clears her throat.*

BABY DOLL:

(*Uneasily*)

Yes, they are poems of nature, Aunt Rose, there is no doubt about it, they are. And, Aunt Rose—while we are talking—step over here for a minute so I can speak to you.

AUNT ROSE *had started away from the porch, as if with a premonition of danger. She stops, her back to the porch, and the fear is visible in her face. It is a familiar fear, one that is graven into her very bones, but which she has never become inured to.*

AUNT ROSE:

What is it, honey?

*She turns around slowly.*

I know you children are feeling upset about something. It don't take a gypsy with cards to figure that out. You an' Archie Lee both are upset about something. I think you were both unsatisfied with your supper. Isn't that it, Baby Doll? The greens didn't boil long enough. Don't you think I know that?

*She looks from* BABY DOLL's *face to* ARCHIE LEE's *back with a hesitant laugh.*

I played a fool trick with my stove, I thought it was lighted and all that time it was . . .

BABY DOLL:

Aunt Rose, won't you set down so we can talk comfortably?

AUNT ROSE:

(*With a note of hysteria*)

I don't want to set down, I don't want to set down, I can talk on my feet! I tell you, getting up an' down is more trouble than it's worth! Now what is it, honey? As soon as I've put these in water, I'm going to light up my stove an' cook you two children some eggs Birmingham. Archie Lee, son, you hear that?

ARCHIE LEE:

(*Roughly, his back still turned*)

I don't want eggs Birmingham.

BABY DOLL:

He don't want eggs Birmingham and neither do I. But while we are talking, Aunt Rose—well—Archie Lee's wondered and I've been wondering, too . . .

AUNT ROSE:

About what, Baby Doll?

BABY DOLL:

Well, as to whether or not you've—made any plans.

AUNT ROSE:

Plans?

BABY DOLL:

Yes, plans.

AUNT ROSE:

What kind of plans, Baby Doll?

BABY DOLL:

Why, plans for the future, Aunt Rose.

AUNT ROSE:

Oh! Future! No—no, when an old maid gets to be nearly a hundred years old, the future don't seem to require much planning for, honey. Many's a time I've wondered but I've never doubted. . . .

*Her voice dies out and there is a strain of music as she faces away from the porch.*

I'm not forgotten by Jesus! No, my Sweet Saviour has not forgotten about me! The time isn't known to me or to you, Baby Doll, but it's known by Him and when it comes He will call me. A wind'll come down and lift me an' take me away! The way that it will the roses when they're like I am. . . .

*The music dies out and she turns back to the tribunal on the front porch.*

BABY DOLL:

(*Clearing her throat again*)

That's all very well, Aunt Rose, to trust in Jesus, but we've got to remember that Jesus only helps those that —well—help themselves!

AUNT ROSE:

Oh, I know that, Baby Doll!

*She laughs.*

Why, I learned that in my cradle, I reckon I must have learned that before I was born. Now when have I ever been helpless? I could count my sick days, the days that I haven't been up and around, on my fingers! My Sweet Saviour has kept me healthy an' active, active an' healthy, yes, I do pride myself on it, my age hasn't made me a burden! And when the time comes that I have to lean on His shoulder, I—

ARCHIE LEE *turns about roughly*

ARCHIE LEE:

All this talk about Jesus an' greens didn't boil an' so forth has got nothing at all to do with the situation! Now look here, Aunt Rose—

BABY DOLL:

(*Getting up*)

Archie Lee, will you hold your tongue for a minute?

ARCHIE LEE:

Then you talk up! And plain! What's there to be so pussyfooting about?

BABY DOLL:

There's ways and there's ways of talking anything over!

ARCHIE LEE:

Well, talk it over and get off the subject of Jesus! There's Susie, there's Jim, there's Tom and Jane and there's Bunny! And if none of them suits her, there's homes in the county will take her! Just let her decide on which one she is ready to visit. First thing in the morning I'll pile her things in the car and drive her out to whichever one's she's decided! Now ain't that a simple procedure compared to all of this pussyfooting around? Aunt Rose has got sense. She's counted the rooms in this house! She knows that I'm nervous, she knows that I've got work to do and a workingman's got to be fed! And his house is his house and he wants it the way that he wants it! Well, Jesus Almighty, if that's not a plain, fair and square way of settling the matter, I'll wash my hands clean and leave you two women to talk it over yourselves! Yes, I'll—be God damned if—!

*He rushes in and slams the screen door. There is a long pause in which* BABY DOLL *looks uncomfortably at nothing, and* AUNT ROSE *stares at the screen door.*

AUNT ROSE:

(*Finally*)

I thought you children were satisfied with my cooking.

*A blue dusk has gathered in the yard.* AUNT ROSE *moves away from the porch and there is a strain of music. The music is drowned out by the catlike whine of the wind turning suddenly angry.* BABY DOLL *gets up from her wicker chair.*

BABY DOLL:

Archie Lee, Archie Lee, you help me in with these chairs before they blow over!

*She drags her chair to the screen door.*

It looks and sounds like a twister! Hold that screen open for me! Pull in that chair! Now this one! We better get down in the cellar!

*As an afterthought.*

Aunt Rose, come in here so we can shut this door!

AUNT ROSE *shakes her head slightly. Then she looks toward the sky, above and beyond the proscenium, where something portentous is forming.* BABY DOLL *back in the house.*

Call Aunt Rose in!

ARCHIE LEE:

The stubborn old thing won't budge.

*The door slams shut. The whine of the angry cat turns into a distant roar and the roar approaches. But* AUNT ROSE *remains in the yard, her face still somberly but quietly thoughtful. The loose gray calico of her dress begins to whip and tug at the skeleton lines of her figure. She looks wonderingly at the sky, then back at the house beginning to shrink into darkness, then back at the sky from which the darkness is coming, at each with the same unflinching but troubled expression. Nieces and nephews and cousins, like pages of an album, are rapidly turned through her mind, some of them loved as children but none of them really her children and all of them curiously unneedful of the devotion that she had offered so freely, as if she had always carried an armful of roses that no one had ever offered a vase to receive. The flimsy gray scarf is whipped away from her shoulders. She makes an awkward gesture and sinks to her knees. Her arms let go of the roses. She reaches vaguely after them. One or two she catches. The rest blow away. She struggles back to her feet. The blue dusk deepens to purple and the purple to black and the roar comes on with the force of a locomotive as* AUNT ROSE'S *figure is still pushed toward the rose bush.*